Dedicated to the memory of my father,
Jim Evans,
who worked at life and whose life worked.

Thankyou

Where does one draw the line to start thanking people when one reaches
a way-station on the journey of life?

Well my line starts and stops with my muse, Aideen.
There would be no book without her. She heard the book when it was
ideas and then, as it began to materialise, she listened as I read my daily
work. She provided many commas, discarded many paragraphs and
fixed much. Whenever I was stuck aloft in a hurricane of doubt she talked
me down. For all the midnight discussions on the finer points of
management, for all the car journeys shining with ideas, for all the
wisdom that brought my thinking into focus, for being my editor, my
partner, my companion, my consolation, my light, my inspiration and my
greatest friend, thank you:
I hope the book justifies your belief in me. You have encouraged me to
dream and then helped those dreams come true. Our daughters, our life
and now this oldest of my dreams, a book with my name on the cover.

I talk about great teachers in my book. Of those I have had many.

My parents who never took life for granted and who taught me to think.
My mother's artistic soul; my father's wisdom, kindness and acceptance.

To all the other explorers, adventurers and teachers mentioned
throughout my book that have inspired and helped me, my thanks.

To the amazing people I have worked, played, argued and explored with
throughout my life, my ongoing gratitude.

Mike and Jamie, thank you both for helping me turn a manuscript into a
book and for being such good friends throughout.

Wyatt, thank you for your generosity, mind and heart.

To you, the reader, my greatest thanks and fondest wishes.

The Trousers of Reality

How to find balance and satisfaction
in life, work and play.

Volume One: Working Life

Why things like
*Agile, Lean, NLP, Systems Thinking
and Theory of Constraints*
are essential for effective project management.

Barry Evans

MBCS CEng CITP

Code Green Publishing
Coventry, UK

ISBN 978-1-907215-00-1

Editor: Aideen Breen

Technical Editors: Mike Boxwell and Jamie Evans

All illustrations by the Author unless otherwise stated
Cover design by Code Green Publishing

Version 1.1

Published by Code Green Publishing
www.codegreenpublishing.com

Foreword

by Wyatt Woodsmall Ph.D.

The Trousers of Reality is an amazing book. It is full of wisdom that anyone can immediately use to improve their lives. The author Barry Evans has the unique distinction of being a Trainer of Neuro Linguistic Programming and a master of software development and business and project management consulting. He is also an accomplished carpenter and builder and has an amazing ability to explain complex concepts in terms of simple everyday experiences that we all share. This unique combination of skills enables him to make cross disciplinary connections which both enhance the disciplines and enrich our lives with new understandings.

This book is based on a set of meta principles that apply to special disciplines but, even more important; apply to all of our daily lives. Wisdom does not consist of a set of detailed instructions and procedures for life but, instead, of a collection of general principles that provide guidance in all situations and contexts. This is what makes this book so powerful and relevant. It speaks to each of us where we are and provides principles that allow us to orient ourselves and to make wise choices on our daily paths.

This book also makes an important and substantial contribution to three disciplines. The first of these is Neuro Linguistic Programming (NLP). NLP is a behavioral science change technology that can be applied to business, education, personal growth, therapy and, most important, to everyday life. NLP is a practical discipline which is based on sound scientific principles. Tragically not all NLP practitioners follow the scientific path and many deviate into what I despairingly call "woo-woo NLP." The Trousers of Reality is an outstanding example of scientific NLP and shows conclusively that NLP is a practical tool and an outcome based discipline. Further NLP when properly taught begins with general scientific concepts and principles and then moves to processes and techniques. Tragically many NLP books focus on techniques and procedures and ignore the fundamental principles that explain why these techniques work. The Trousers of Reality takes the other path and focuses on the general principles which make NLP practices effective in a wide range of practical circumstances.

NLP is based on models of what successful experts actually do. Barry Evans has done a remarkable job of applying NLP to four disciplines that are critically important as we advance into the 21st century. These are software development and design, systems thinking, project management and business management in general. I am excited and gratified to see NLP through this book have a powerful positive influence on these disciplines. It is particularly gratifying to see a way that NLP can be used in these rigorous disciplines. This book is both a tool and a master coach and training in NLP and the other disciplines.

This book also makes a major contribution to the latest developments in software development. It takes technical concepts and models such as Agile, Lean, TOC, and Systems Thinking and both explains what they mean and, more significantly, how we can all benefit from understanding these powerful concepts and models.

One reason that Barry Evans is such a powerful teacher is his use of metaphor as a way to explain. It is easy to get lost in complex explanations and technical jargon. Metaphors connect to our experiences and allow us to focus on the big picture instead of drowning in the details. This book is an outstanding example of how NLP should be taught. Just reading this book will help people in all walks of life because of the amount of perception-enhancing language patterns it contains.

The Trousers of Reality goes far beyond NLP and IT. It is visionary and fresh and new. It is for everyone who wants to set themselves free from the constrained thinking of tribalism and labels. It is a creative use of NLP in the teaching of IT methodologies, planning and problem solving. Furthermore, all of these disciplines have meta principles which converge with each other and with life. Discovering these meta principles is like finding the marrow of life. Learning anything throws new light on everything else. We all need this book. Read it, listen to it, let it speak to you. It can change your life for the better.

Wyatt Woodsmall, Ph.D.
is a Master Trainer, Master Coach and Master Modeler in NLP. He is a co-founder of the International NLP Trainers Association. He has trained in 26 countries on 5 continents. He is the co-author of 3 books on NLP. His web sites are:

www.thescienceofidiots.com
and
www.inlpta.org

A note from the author

I set out to throw out the bathwater but keep the baby. I set out to write a book that will take something as complex as Software Development and talk about it in a way that would interest those involved in the field and those who are reading about it from curiosity.

To do this I realised that I would need to explain the web of connections I see. Like Winnie the Pooh I am a being of simple brain. I hope that it is the simplicity that comes at the other side of complexity.

Evolution may look complex but it is a simple process. That which works survives. Not only does it survive but it proliferates. Those things that are refined and which match purpose, ability and execution come together in simple combinations upon which great complexity can be built.

The older the foundation, the simpler it is. In biology, physics and chemistry the building blocks are astoundingly simple and almost laughably coincidental. Roll them back and they obey the same laws.

Keep pushing those simple laws beyond this point you will find complexity lies at the other side. Push past the relationship between light, energy and matter, push past the atom to the hidden world beneath the neat principles, as today's scientists do, and you will find complexity on the other side again. The very big and the very small are equally mysterious.

Like a möbius strip or an infinity symbol there is a point of convergence - a crossroads of simplicity – a balance point. That which can attain this simplicity from chaos and upon which great things can be built is where you will find illumination.

It is the crossroads that make the journey interesting, it is the point of choice where power lies and where reality converges, it is diversity that draws us to one another.

I have written four volumes, of which this is the first. This book deals with why the things that work do work and why you need to find them and use them.

The Second volume deals with what you can do with the principles that work. It explores the purposes for which you can use them.

The third volume talks about how specifically you can use them to achieve these things. It draws together the applications and how you can practically apply them.

The fourth take things further examines some of the basic issues that face relationships, our society and our world. It looks at what a master craftsman might be able to do and how you can deal with any situation.

Being male I have used the male pronoun by default throughout this book. Please read into this only that I found it easier to write this way. Sexual equality is one of the principles I have based my career and life upon.

Table of Contents

Prelude

In the year 60 AD Hero of Alexandria built a robot[1]. He used logic which resembles modern computer language. He had already built a steam powered engine one and a half millennia before it was formally invented.

In the year 1492 the Spanish Inquisition was established. The authorities in Europe opposed rational thought and were seeing witchcraft and heresy in every corner of their world. The bright flares of the civilisations of Ancient Greece and Rome had been burned out for more than a thousand years.

In 1634 the son of a musician was under house arrest for saying the world orbited the sun. The Roman Inquisition was accusing him of the heresy of disputing the literal truth of the bible. Legend has it his final word on the matter was "And yet it moves"[2] in reference to the planet he walked upon. His father had taught him maths through music.

In 1642 a mind was born prematurely into a tiny body that could fit in a quart cup. As it grew it observed. From those observations this mind explained all motion, including the motions of the planets, in three sentences[3]. This mind gave birth to a scientific revolution and is considered to have made the greatest overall contribution to scientific thinking and to be one of the greatest ever benefactors of humankind[4]. This greatest of rational minds and the father of modern science was also the mind of an alchemist.

---

1 http://www.newscientist.com/blog/technology/2007/07/programmab le-robot-from-60ad.html
2 "Eppur si muove". Gilileo is reputed to have said this as he signed his recantation.
3 The laws of motion. Also see Philosophiæ Naturalis Principia Mathematica (mathematical principles of natural philosophy) the three volume work of Isaac Newton
4 http://royalsociety.org/news.asp?id=3880

In 1955 an intellect that had electrified the world with insights into the very fabric of the universe was laid to rest. An old gentleman had died in his sleep. His name in his own lifetime had become synonymous with genius. He gave the world its greatest insight into the nature of the universe and, much to his dismay; he also gave it its greatest means of destruction. Such is the nature of knowledge and truth. He had deduced that spacetime is curved and that matter and energy are the same thing. He claimed that his imagination was the most powerful scientific tool he had. He played the violin to help him think. He overturned 200 years of status quo by posing beautiful questions. He had solved the riddle of relativity by daydreaming he was riding on a beam of sunlight[5].

Long before any of this in the year 212 BC a Greek was killed by a Roman soldier. The soldier killed him because he was able to. He reasoned that being able to, gave him the right. The man he murdered was able to move the whole earth with a stick and a stone and a good place to stand[6]. Legend has it that his last words were "Do not disturb my circles" referring to a mathematical problem he was working on. Patterns were lost that would not start fully emerging again until that night in 1642.

---

5 http://www.amnh.org/exhibitions/einstein/light/revolution.php
6 "Give me but one firm spot on which to stand, and I will move the earth."- Archimedes of Syracuse
The Oxford Dictionary of Quotations, Second Edition, Oxford University Press, London, 1953, p. 14

In a nutshell

This book explores the knowledge and wisdom of 3000 years. It shows how the discoveries of the great philosophers and scientists are about what you do every day.

It proposes that there is a root and branch to excellence and that skills distilled in one context can be transferred to another.

As a case study it focuses on the transfer of skills between programming software and Management. It shows that the deep principles, that make both work, are reciprocal.

Art, philosophy, psychology, history, science, music and DIY are explored in a search for principles that work.

It shows you how to discover why they work and how to apply all of the skills you might have however you came by them.

This book is for you if you would like to understand how to make best use of all of the resources available to you.

It is aimed at those who see life, both work and play, as an amazing opportunity to achieve excellence and find meaning in every breath.

This book will not teach you to think outside the box. It will make you question the existence of boxes.

Themes, directions and koans

"The time has come,"
The Walrus said
"To talk of many things:"
Alice Through The Looking Glass
- Charles Lutwidge Dodgson

The Trousers of Reality

There is no such thing as an intractable problem.

This bold statement takes courage to utter. To live your life by it and to stake your professional reputation on it takes the proof of experience. It also takes a little qualification.

All problems are solvable as long as you are prepared to change your perspective and challenge your assumptions and the assumptions of all those around you.

My brother once got hopelessly lost on a road trip. When he finally found his way to his destination he opened a bottle of wine and settled down to examine the map. A map he had not had in the car.

"Ah, I see", he said looking at the point at which he had gone wrong on the motorway; "I went down the wrong leg of the trousers".

Ever since that comment I have seen all decisions as a matter of negotiating the trousers of reality.

A koan is a question or a thought exercise designed to make you think differently about something. This book is intended to be koan and the next page contains the first nested koan.

Reciprocity and Balance

Reality has a cornerstone. Reciprocity here means the equivalence of ideas, of actions and of things. It is also called consequence. It is implemented through the art of balance. It relies on feedback.

Universality and Context

Is something meaningful because of its content or because of its communication? Universality here means the hierarchy and applicability of ideas, of actions and of things. It is also called perspective. It is implemented through the art of context. It relies on sequence.

Longevity and Inspiration

A marathon is won with stamina. Longevity here means the durability and flexibility of ideas, of actions and of things. It is also called sustainability. It is implemented through the art of inspiration. It relies on repeatability.

Evolution and Interconnectedness

Riddle reality with possibility. Evolution here means the fluidity and mutability of ideas, of actions and of things. It is also called feedback. It is implemented through the art of making connections. It relies on choice.

> In this book I use software development and project management as a metaphor to explore the idea that there are things that sometimes work and principles that always work. I use both "Developer" and "Programmer" to refer to Software Engineers.

Interconnectedness

I have been working for all of my adult life. I have worked in different companies and in the public and private sector. I have worked in different countries and in different professions. I have also been alive for all that time. As a human being I have done what all of us do which is to observe. I have a compulsion to learn and to make connections.

Sometimes it is hard not to believe that there is a basic interconnectedness to everything. Let me explain.

Everything that has ever happened to you, everything that is happening to you, everything that will ever happen to you is interconnected. All these moments, events, thoughts, tears, laughter, victories, defeats, friendships, loves, enemies, friends, places and times have one thing in common:

You!

All of these things are interconnected because they are the things that are on the path that you cut through time and space. None of us are casual observers. Even if we believe we are not taking any action, our very presence affects the balance.

Context

Context[7] tells us about the environment in which we are operating. It gives meaning to the concepts we are balancing. It is the main ingredient in lateral thinking and problem solving.

---

7 Context Analysis = SWOT: Strength, Weakness, Opportunity, Threat. It is a pretty blunt instrument but it can be useful in the right context.

If you understand what context you are in you can use it as sailors used the sun. You can use it to calculate your latitude in any situation. The calculation of the longitude, or where you are in the situation, relies on an appreciation of the concentric circles of hierarchy.

Hierarchy was originally invented by the church to describe the levels of angels. This was right before they started arguing about how many could dance on the head of a pin.

Hierarchy is not a measure of importance as I speak about it here. It is a level of detail. It is a level of perspective. I use context and hierarchy as x and y coordinates. As with Cartesian coordinates we need a third axis to give meaning in the higher dimensions. With this we can provide inspiration.

Balance

There is a great deal of interest in change. Many people ask themselves whether they should embrace it or resist it. At what point does one thing change into another? When is change good and how do we know? Where, in the grey, does black turn into white?

Malcolm Gladwell[8] has interested the world in the "tipping point"; how little things can make a big difference. Gregory Bateson[9] talked about the difference that makes a difference; the information that allows us to distinguish one thing from another.

Where is the zenith in the arc of the pendulum? Have you

8 Malcolm Gladwell: Author and pop psychologist most famous for the books "The Tipping Point", "Blink" and "Outliers".

9 Gregory Bateson (1904-80): Anthropologist, linguist, scientist. Helped establish the science of Cybernetics (the study of feedback). Deeply involved in Systems Theory and the study of epistemology.

ever thrown a ball high into the air and watched as it stops, balanced between the going up and the coming down? Have you ever noticed that there is a moment where all the forces acting on it are in balance? It is the moment of greatest stillness and of greatest change? This paradox is delightful.

There is a strange philosophical idea that motion should be impossible. The distance between two points can be halved infinitely. You have to pass all of these halves in order to move between the two points. It should take infinitely long to traverse an infinity. ***Eppur si muove***. And yet we move.

There are physical rules to the universe that usher all things toward equilibrium. There are no conflicts in nature. All things to flow toward equilibrium. Water always flows downhill. Put two containers of water beside each other with a hose between them and they will find the same level[10].

Electricity works because of the entropic desire of nature to smooth the potential difference between joined poles. Potential difference makes the electrons flow[11]. Heat is the energy flowing from more agitated molecules to less agitated molecules.

It surprised early scientists to discover that heat is not a

---

10 You will have to start the syphoning process in order to join the areas of imbalance. Sometimes things remain in imbalance unless something joins them and allows the flow to happen.

11 I have always found it interesting that electrons flow in the opposite direction to electricity. Potential difference is a lack or electrons. Because electrons are negatively charged lack of them leads to a positive charge and electrons flow out of anything into the positive charge. When you get a shock it is not something called electricity flowing into you, it is electrons flowing out of you. By the same token lightening is electrons from the earth smashing up into the sky but we perceive fire coming down. If you do not find this fascinating you need a shock to the system to get yourself going again.

substance but that it is an energy imbalance correcting itself.

If you examine pressure, it is easier to appreciate that the forces are all about equalisation. Thermodynamics is the ghost in the machine that helps the universe to exist.

Entropy is the measure of disorder of the system. In systems, entropy is the measure of the systems energy not available to do work. In other words - its potential.

When we talk about entropy, work and order; balance is the thing that gives it context.

Inspiration

Inspiration is the vital ingredient. Most companies seek to motivate. What they do not understand is that in seeking to motivate they achieve the opposite.

W Edwards Deming[12] strictly prohibited motivation. He was right. When people feel that they are being motivated they accept it as criticism. To suggest that they need motivation is to suggest that they need to be driven, prodded or coaxed. The effect is to demotivate people.

This is a bad habit to get people into. It leads to dependence at best and deliberate sabotage by the disgruntled at worst.

Based on the observation of a quarter of a century, working with people from all over the world in a variety of professional settings, I have found that a theory Y[13] model of the business world works. It is an optimistic model but a practical one.

What many of us fear in others is the reflection of our own weakness. We can associate the behaviours of others with things we do not like about ourselves.

This is not as bad as you might think. It is the dark side of a coin that has a very bright side indeed.

Firstly, good and bad are all relative. Many people are simply

---

12 D W Edwards Deming was a statistician who increased productivity in the USA during the second world war and who is revered in Japan as a hero. His ideas were used to create the huge successes in Japanese manufacturing. His theories are the basis for Lean manufacturing.

13 Based on the work of Douglas McGregor there are two theories of management. Theory X is based on mistrust and the need for supervision. Theory Y is based on bringing out a natural desire to do a good job, be creative and accept responsibility.

too hard on themselves and in turn they are too hard on others.

Some or the hardest people to work for are people who have an over-developed work ethic. They set their own standards so high and drive themselves so hard that they lose perspective on the needs and wishes of others.

Secondly, the fact that we can recognise potential for improvement in ourselves is a strength. If you are pragmatic and reasonable then this should encourage you. You have self knowledge and you have the potential ability to engage in generative learning. This is learning that allows us to change our behaviour and our responses.

The third is that with the same insight we can also see our good qualities in others. Sometimes these may still only be potential good qualities that we would like to cultivate in ourselves. The point is that we can recognise them and aspire to them.

We can be inspired by others who have the qualities we want because we can see that these qualities are possible. We are capable of admiration for our friends and colleagues who have skill and integrity; stamina and fair-mindedness; fortitude and kindness; wisdom and patience; taste and character; will and compassion.

Look inside yourself and the best you find there exists in the people around you too. I rely on it, so do you. We all want the best in ourselves to be recognised, to be enough and to triumph.

A word about sociopaths:

A Person who has no conscience and who is unconcerned with the adverse consequences of their actions on others may be termed a sociopath. Apparently 4% of the male and 1% of the female population are sociopaths[14] .

They are hard to spot in business because they are almost always charming. You must learn to recognise then because the normal rules of behaviour and management do not apply.

The fourth and final volume in this series, entitled "The Other Game", will deal explicitly with this.

For now be aware that this type of behaviour is tolerated to a frightening degree and often rewarded in our culture, making us believe that there are many more of these people than there actually are.

Of course there are sociopaths out there in the world and so I am suggesting that we keep a hefty lump of common sense about us while we keep them in perspective.

The vast, overwhelming majority of people I have encountered have been, in one way or another, heroes. We seek out fellow travellers and companions and learn how to trust them. Can you imagine what it would be to inspire someone as you have been inspired?

Each of us is a Hero on a quest to write our story.

---

14 http://www.bbc.co.uk/blogs/thereporters/markeaston/2008/11/spotting _a_sociopath.html.

The Most Important Chapter In This Book

"For now we see through a glass, darkly."
1 Corinthians 13:12

Deep structure and surface structure

Deep structure is what we mean. Surface structure is what we say[15].

This is certainly the key to getting along with other people. It is the nature of knowledge. It is why Newton and Einstein are both right. It is why both your children are telling the truth when one says white and the other says black.

In computer systems, data is held in databases. It is held in a structured format that allows the database to work at a deep level with the data. It allows us to store and use phenomenal amounts of data and search through it in fractions of seconds.

When we design systems we present this data according to the requirement of the different systems sharing the database.

If we were to present data as it is stored in the database, we would have to create a new database for every application. This would result in a huge amount of wastage[16]. Fortunately we can present this data in an almost infinite number of ways, because we have separated storage and presentation.

If you were to show an application to a systems developer he

---

15 This, not 42, may very well be the ultimate answer. In Douglas Adams' "Hitch Hikers Guide to the Galaxy" a computer called "Deep Thought" is built to find the ultimate answer. It declares the answer to be 42 but neither Deep Thought nor its makers know what the question is. It is, therefore, useless information.
16 In fact this is how it used to be done up until the advent of multi-tier systems where the data, the logic and the presentation are separated.

might have an educated guess at how the data might be stored. Even an experienced developer would need to see a lot of systems, and how they use the data, in order to even make a guess about the deep structure of the data.

A non systems person would not have a clue. In fact many people who use systems assume that the data is held as it is presented to them. They have no reason to care about how it is stored.

When we talk to each other we use language to communicate what is in our mind. This language is the presentation of the data from our internal database. This database is the repository for all of our experiences, learning, attitudes, values, beliefs and perceptions. It is composed of memories, conditioned responses, prejudices, social responses and strategies.

Were I to say the word "Orange" to you, it might mean the fruit, the colour, a political affiliation or a fizzy drink. You may mishear me and think I said "arrange", which could be to tidy, to plan something or to write music. You may think I was talking about a place where cattle are at home, a fireplace, somewhere to fire weapons, a distance and so on.

The context provides crucial clues. Even so....

If I were to say to the doctor that I have a pain in my stomach, you might think the meaning would be quite clear. A good doctor will ask me what sort of pain it is. Is it sharp, aching, stinging, throbbing, stabbing, dull or otherwise? I may use one of the above descriptions and say sharp. Then does sharp mean the same thing to both of us?

There is every chance the doctor would perceive the same pain as stabbing. Stabbing might be how the doctor would describe what I perceive as throbbing. Throbbing might be how someone else would describe what I feel as dull.

There is an inescapable conclusion here that we live in a world of our own perceptions and that we really have very little idea of what anybody else really feels.

When we talk to others, we map their words on to our own experience. For the most part this works pretty well because we seem to get the general gist.

There is a deep structure and a surface structure. The deep structure is what you are thinking and feeling. The surface structure is how you express it. Deep structure is what we mean. Surface structure is what we say.

It would be too laborious if everyday language had to be precise enough to describe everything in accurate detail exactly as we mean it. Instead we use metaphor and shared cultural experience to approximate what we mean. This is enough for us to get along - most of the time.

So, if we accept that we each have a deep structure, which is what we mean, then we can also accept that different people will interpret what we say depending on their own deep structure. Sometimes these deep structures are called subjective models. Everyone has their own subjective model through which they interpret all of their experiences and communications.

Let's just talk about you and me right now in order to simplify it all a bit.

I can express my deep structure in a number of ways. It is like the presentation of the data from the database on to a web page. The presentation depends on the structure of the web page not of the data. You have the ability to present your internal data in different ways.

Even if we do agree that we are talking about the same thing, our internal representation or associations may be different. I might say Blackpool and see a dreary English seaside town where I spent a fortnight one day. You might say Blackpool and see a great place full of charming tearooms where you spent the best holiday of your life with your favourite friend.

In this way there is a many to many relationship. Deep structures to surface structures.

A deep structure may map to many surface structures. A surface structure may map to many deep structures.

Gravity

If we admit the existence of subjective models of the world we might start to ask about objective models. We wonder what might really be there.

I think we may assume that the theory of gravity is a safe enough place to find agreement. What goes up must come down. Mustn't it? It is much more of a constant experience for all of us than, let's say, time, for instance.

There is a deep structure and surface structure to gravity. There is a deep structure and a surface structure to just about everything. Many of the following chapters are built on this principle.

Galileo starts our story of the uncovering of the deep structure of gravity. He dropped some weights from the leaning Tower of Pisa. He noticed that, regardless of the weight, things took the same time to reach the ground. Up until then most people thought it was common sense that heavier things fell faster.

The surface structure of gravity indicated that this was the case. A deeper understanding showed that it was air resistance that made the difference between things like feathers and marbles. Galileo theorised that gravity has a constant acceleration, which is approximately 10 meters per second per second.

We, the people who care about it, then thought we understood gravity pretty well. It is something that makes things fall and it is constant. QED. What more do you need to know? Open and shut case. Gravity signed sealed and delivered.

Newton continues the story. He peeled back the seal and he recognised that there was more deep structure there to be savoured. He proved mathematically that gravity was a universal constant relative to the mass of objects and the distance between their centres. $F=GMm/R^2$.

Roughly speaking everything with mass in the universe exerts a gravitational force on everything else with mass. This theory explained the orbits of planets in the solar system. It eventually predicted the existence of Neptune because of observed movements of the planet Uranus.

For two hundred years this stood as the definitive explanation of gravity. Except for the planet Mercury, of course. Mercury is the closest planet to the sun and its orbit does not behave as it should, according to Newton.

Most of Newton's followers in the scientific establishment spent a lot of time looking for another planet. This would explain everything and bring Mercury's orbit back under Newton's laws. This had been the case with the orbit of the planet Uranus after all - Newton's laws implied the presence of another gravitational body and it had appeared, had it not? Mercury remained a puzzle though. Nobody could find the elusive hidden planet.

When Einstein cast the searchlight of his intellect towards the deep structure, he uncovered the theory of relativity, complete with its notions of spacetime curvature. There was outrage in certain quarters. This would disprove Newton and that just would not do! Newton had to be right. It was the surface structure we were comfortable with.

Prove it Einstein did, though. He also explained the orbit of Mercury without another planet. Now the deep structure was looking a lot different and it was heading away from the surface structure at light speed.

Did Einstein prove Newton wrong though?

Well, he proved that Newton's surface theory did not fully explain the deep structure. Newton's laws still hold for non-relativistic gravity calculations. You will also find that Galileo's 10m/s/s will do you for most calculations you have to make about gravity in your life.

Einstein's theories are so convincing as a good explanation of the deep structure that you may be startled when I refer to them as another surface structure. Einstein's theories do not seem to explain some of the phenomena of Quantum Physics.

Every surface structure, by its nature, is incomplete. The more accurate and consistent it is the more it points to another surface structure. To quote Stephen King: "The pillar of truth has a hole in it". In other words, all understanding is theory. If it purports to be the "truth", it has to be a lie. A good theory will always ask more questions than it answers. It will always open doors to discovering different views of the deep structure. It will open the doors of knowledge.

Quantum physicists are now considering string theory and M theory to explain gravity. Apparently spacetime may have at least 11 dimensions. That which we perceive to be reality is only what protrudes into our dimensions. It includes the holographic principle[17].

This holographic principle interests me, although my understanding of the physics is limited. It appears to assert that what we perceive as reality is a shadow cast from another dimension[18]. Cast from a fifth dimension onto our four like a shadow cast on the four walls of a room.

String theory and M Theory, although completely theoretical at present, do seem to subsume and allow all the preceding theories.

Plato's allegory of the cave told a story of people chained in a cave. They are chained so that they can only see shadows cast on the wall by the fire. Some of them escape and get out of the cave. When they come back and try to explain what they have seen they are considered to be lunatics by their friends.

Lao Tzu, the great Chinese philosopher, says that knowledge gets in the way of understanding. I have always felt instinctively that this is correct but it did not appear to sit well with my conviction that learning is the greatest of all endeavours. Neither does it appear to sit well with Bateson's assertion that knowledge is what solves the mind body problem by linking the map and the territory. Then I thought of Eddington.

---

17 Worth some time and research if you are interested
18 I have by necessity vastly oversimplified even what I understand here.

Eddington wrote to Einstein and asked him about the orbit of Mercury. Einstein, having been asked the right question, went on to show that the behaviour of Mercury could be explained by his theory of space curvature close to a gravitational body the size of the sun.

Eddington then proceeded to prove Einstein was right. He photographed stars around the sun during a solar eclipse and compared them to photographs of the same part of the sky when it could be seen at night.

The stars around the sun were in slightly different positions. This proved that the presence of the sun was curving space and bending light. The conclusion was that Einstein must be right about spacetime, relativity and gravity.

What makes Eddington's contribution so extraordinary was that, as assistant to the astronomer royal at the Greenwich Observatory, he was a respected scientist of a very Newtonian persuasion. He had to let the assumptions of 200 years go, in order to understand Einstein. Had he let his knowledge cloud his thinking, we might never have heard of Einstein.

In effect, he realised that his knowledge was a surface structure. He realised that although Einstein's theories may have appeared contradictory to all sanity, they were part of another surface structure. He was able to grasp that both of the surface structures were reflecting the same deep structure.

The Globe

Imagine any field of knowledge. Imagine it is a dark glass globe. Imagine that at its centre is the thing itself. It casts reflections on the inside of the sphere. Imagine that you have to work very hard to scrape a pinprick size viewing hole to see that reflection. The reflection is two dimensional. It is an image of the thing at the centre reflected on the surface of the globe. It is a surface structure.

Now imagine that you, and everyone else, are looking through a series of lenses of your own. Some people have coloured and distorted lenses or lenses with bits blacked out. When you look at the surface structure you all report truthfully about what you see. You are seeing part of a two dimensional image of a three dimensional object projected on a curved surface of a darkened globe. You are also each seeing it through a set of highly personalised lenses. Then you start to argue.

Now imagine you go to a different place on the sphere and scrape another little peep hole. This time the image cast is quite different.

If you are one type of fool, you treat this as an epiphany that means everything you thought you knew was wrong and, at last, you know the truth now.

If you are another type of fool, you pretend you did not see it or that it is something else. You just ignore it altogether.

In either case you only have room for one pin hole's worth of knowledge about anything.

If you are wise, you start to comprehend that what is at the centre may be completely different to what you first thought it was. You realise that what you saw in the first peep- hole was a true reflection from that angle; just as this new view is a true reflection from this new angle.

You realise that that the views are not contradictory, your assumptions were. Accordingly you start feverishly to scratch peep-holes everywhere you can.

Newton was able to see through many pinholes and was able to clearly describe what he saw. Einstein looked through different pinholes and saw some more.

Newton would probably have been most excited by Einstein and his theories; but to me Eddington is one of the true intellectual heroes. He removed his protective lenses, even if only for a moment, and dared the naked light, literally staring at the stars beside the eclipsed sun.

The exploration of the atom for many years consisted of firing things at speed into atoms and looking at the resulting scatter pattern on photographic plates. We look at stars in deep space by spectrograph analysis of the light from them to see what's in them.

When you know that the things on the wall are shadows, you start being able to make deductions about their true nature.

When you realise that what you understand is the surface structure, you can start to imagine the possibilities of the deep structure.

Sometimes we make the wrong deductions. a=b, b=c => a=c. Swans are white, sheep are white, swans are sheep.

Principles are transparent. They are atomic and carry information only about themselves. They do not make assumptions. They clarify. They simplify.

Principles are like really good spy-holes on the deep structure of something. They reveal a surface structure that is consistent with all other known surface structures.

They are usually discovered by people whose own lenses are

relatively clear.

Perhaps the spyhole is a little larger than normal? Perhaps principles come about when someone has seen the deep structure from a number of angles and has made a correct deduction about some aspect of the deep structure?

Principles, by nature, are decoupled from any one single surface structure.

Even science is only one way of making pinholes. It is a vastly superior way because of the way we try to test what we see against the other pinholes we have. We get some workable principles this way.

Sometimes we perceive the deep structure and we call it intuition or flashes of insight. We have discovered a perspective that allows us to penetrate the inner structure.

In volume two of this work I will talk in particular about this phenomenon and how to train intuition and differentiate it from wishful thinking.

Interpreting the shadows on the wall

If you accept the idea of deep and surface structure in communications and knowledge, there are things you can start to understand about work and about life.

You begin to understand that people behave the way they do because they are clinging to a surface structure. They are watching a shadow on the wall of the cave as if it were reality.

You understand that changing perspective is good because it reveals more of the deep structure to you. You understand that people stick to beliefs to the point of war and beyond because they want the world to be as simple as their surface structures. You know that you can communicate better by learning about people's deep structures.

You know that things which are principle based tend to work better because they are less anchored to one surface structure.

You understand that changing perspective is good because you see the deep structure better. You know that the admission of ignorance is the beginning of wisdom. You make room for other points of view. You know that there is no one truth that could possibly explain a deep structure. The only truth is that the deep structure exists.

You know that what you think you know is constructed from your own deductions about swans and sheep. You know why you love to learn and that you are hungry for knowledge. It is because you want to see what is really there. You want to get out of the cave and see the sunlight.

Right and Wrong

This does not mean that everyone is right just because they are accurately reporting their surface structure. If their surface structure does not change it is because they do not change their position. Sometimes they are looking at the reflection through coloured or blacked out lenses. The more surface structures you see the more right you are but you also get to know how much more right you need to be.

Trying to prove someone wrong is ultimately a waste of time, even if it is sometimes fun. They can clearly see the surface structure they are looking at. Seeing another surface structure does not make the first one wrong, but the more surface structures you have seen, the more pinholes you have gazed through, the more complete your understanding will become and the more right you will be. The clearer you can make your own lenses the more you will get from looking at these reflected surface structures.

The paradox is that the more pin holes you have peered through, the more you realise you don't know. The clearer your lens gets the bigger the universe gets. The person with the most knowledge will often profess the greatest ignorance.

This is not humility in the traditional sense. It is the sort of humility you feel while standing in the desert under the night sky as opposed to the arrogance you might feel while driving along a small town road in control of your car with the stereo blasting out your favourite song.

The world can seem deceptively familiar because you have surrounded yourself with walls. In the desert you find out who you are.

"The best thing for being sad," replied Merlin, beginning to puff and blow, "is to learn something. That's the only thing that never fails. You may grow old and trembling in your anatomies, you may lie awake at night listening to the disorder of your veins, you may miss your only love, you may see the world about you devastated by evil lunatics, or know your honour trampled in the sewers of baser minds. There is only one thing for it then - to learn. Learn why the world wags and what wags it. That is the only thing which the mind can never exhaust, never alienate, never be tortured by, never fear or distrust, and never dream of regretting. Learning is the only thing for you. Look what a lot of things there are to learn — pure science, the only purity there is."
The Once and Future King
- T.H. White

The Map

*"When you break the big laws, you do not get liberty;
you do not even get anarchy. You get the small laws."*
G.K.Chesterton

Topography

Think of Einstein and Archimedes. Think of Newton and Galileo. Think of the lever and spaceships. Think of the centuries and millennia behind us. Think of the explorers and cartographers of the human experience who have gone before us into the strange lands of discovery.

Now, if we were to rise up above time and look back along the very time-line from which we have just emerged, what would it be like? While we could appreciate the worries and concerns, triumphs and joy, loss and loves of the millions who have lived, what else would we see?

Would we see patterns? Would we see everything as beginnings to endings, rising and falling, light and darkness, one thing becoming the next? Would it appear to us that things are becoming what they are going to be and simultaneously returning to what they had been in the past? Would we see progress as a straight line or would we see circles from Hero and his steam engine to Watts and his perfect engine?

What would you have to notice in order to make sense of it and understand how we got here; and where we are going?

I do know that there are things that survive. There are some things that have linear survival and others that are lost and rediscovered in cycles. I know that every child that is born will have to learn the world anew. We try to make it easier by writing down what we consider to be really important for them to learn. We get better at teaching and better at understanding the learner with every generation.

There are tools we have been given by minds that went before. They told us how they reasoned them out of nothing and tested them in the flames of intolerance. These are the things which we preserve.

These tools are underlying principles that have been discovered as we evolve. Each of us has to discover them in our own life.

Every age, every job, every circumstance has a fog of details of fads and of fashions. They can serve to distort the underlying principles of clarity of thought. The need is to hand on the wheat and discard the chaff when it has served its purpose.

Meta Rules and software development methodologies

The following uses the IT industry as a practical example and to illustrate the need to distinguish between process and principle.

If companies were to have a shopping list of objectives for a methodology it might look something like this:

✓Ensure that the system is fit for purpose
✓Ensure that the system is complete
✓Ensure that system is compatible with existing systems and business strategy
✓Ensure that the system is affordable and maximum value for money
✓Ensure that the system makes best use of available budget

Even if a project were to be 100% successful in terms of methodology, how effective is your investment if you have spent a large percentage of your budget sustaining that methodology? You want to be sure that you are delivering the right thing.

Many companies deliver the methodology process to applause but the systems never materialise.

Methodologies breed processes, processes breed practices and behaviour. The outcome is limited to the scope and applicability of the process. Fear causes people to cling to the process because they do not want to risk the responsibility associated with independent thought. Flaws in the process are therefore transmitted and replicated.

There is as yet no grand unifying methodology or process at the level of detail we demand in software development. There are a number of reasons for this. Primary among these is that what we do in software development is so complex and that complexity increases in tandem with Moore's law[19].

To cover all the possibilities of this complexity an all encompassing methodology would have to be so detailed that it would be unworkable. Instead methodology creators build in assumptions and constraints.

---

19 Moore's Law and derivatives, roughly stated, say that technology doubles in capacity and speed every two years. This is an exponential increase and so far holds more or less true. Just look at the evolution of digital cameras, memory sticks, laptops etc. year on year to confirm this observation.

Technology and change strain these assumptions and constraints until the methodology process quickly becomes a bottleneck on both creativity and productivity.

Fear of this complexity causes management to demand a grand unifying methodology which will render technology and its acolytes predictable and safe.

In doing so we create a market for methodologies that allows vendors to inflict increasingly totalitarian methodologies aimed at constricting change. They hit their limits faster and faster and are discarded, or ignored, by the development community, with increasing frequency.

With every methodology we discard, or disregard, we make the mistake of throwing away the basic principles they had borrowed. What we should be discarding, and disregarding, are flawed and corrupted interpretations of first principles. Instead we take on a new set of interpretations of other principles, which will, in time, be proved to be ineffective, because things move on and change.

It seems to me looking at the history of all this that there is a flip flopping going on back and forth. Rather than refining and adding the principles to one another, we are doing an "either/or" dance in a crazy pattern. It seems to be because we can not stomach the truth.

Some methodologies claim that principles are the elements of a particular process. This essentially binds the principles to a leaky boat. This is inverse logic and causes very unproductive behaviour. It puts the cart before the horse.

We buy methodologies and processes supported by software products because we are sure the answer lies in high-tech. This generates sloppy thinking across the board.

We need to hire intelligent, skilled people whom we can trust. The truth is that, with the growing complexity of technology and its capabilities, we need these people not to just tell us if it works, but also to tell us whether we need this technology or not.

This infers that you need people who are capable of independent thought, who can think laterally, and who can keep pace with change.

Methodologies are increasingly encouraging command and control behaviour in order to replace expensive workers with cheap labour that can follow a set of instructions. The hope seems to be that if we can get technology to a certain level, it can solve all our problems. Then we will not need genius or expensive employees.

Change usually gives us a different perspective and uncovers distortions, deletions and generalisations. If we resist change in order to keep repeating the same process, we risk not uncovering and correcting these. We can lose connection with the deep structure of the principles.

Many people realise that we are circling the principles. Each attempt to get it right should help us to uncover the deep structure or principles that lie under the surface. These help us to hold on to what is uncovered. We should end up with a refined set of rules that are decoupled from any particular instance.

These generalised rules should become easier to adapt to the particular instance we are dealing with.

A metaphor for this might be a useful tool, like a drill, to which you can fit different bits, depending on whether you are drilling wood, metal or concrete. You could have saw attachments and polishing attachments. The basic circular motion at speed is at the heart and common to the applications.

Throw away what does not work and keep what does. There are false couplings between principles and their applications. We must recognise them. This is the difference between refinement and reductionism.

We either throw away too much or not enough. Like getting a new drill for every material you need to drill (Changing too much); or using lots of wood bits on the brick wall instead of changing to a concrete bit (changing too little but with lots of wasted effort and time).

The first level of skill is to know what to throw away and

what to keep. It is a meta rule: a rule about rules.

For the purposes of clarification when I talk about principles I am talking about meta rules.

Science, cycles, fractals and recursion

Science is based on observation, the serendipity of observation and the patterns that emerge from it. Observation, hypothesis, test, review, confirmation, theory. Elegant.

Yet, will a wheel roll, will a lever move weights, will equality always balance, will distance change perspective whether or not we have a peer review or a theory?

Science is the search for the rule that encapsulates; for the rung we can stand on; for the window with a view. Yet to understand the stars we have had to examine the atom.

There is a circular texture to all great thinking. Circles within circles. Spirals and cones. When one thing goes far enough in either direction it becomes its opposite. East becomes west and west becomes east, day becomes night and night becomes day.

The older we get the more we realise that there does not seem to be linear progression to a happy ending in the way the fairy stories of childhood taught us. The happy ending is being able to accept that change is inevitable, that nothing lasts forever and that this is a good thing.

If we are watching carefully we notice that things happen in cycles and that the nature of life is circular. Planets spin around the sun, the atoms spin around their nuclei, the seasons revolve, happiness gives way to grief and grief gives way to happiness. Even childhood turns to old age and then old age turns to childhood. Laughter turns to tears and tears, brought to their conclusion, turn back to laughter. Everything is only a cycle away from its opposite.

Sometimes, but not always, the opposite is its counterbalance.

Nature is fractal. Examine a tree. Its branches follow the same pattern down to the smallest twig. Are ideas the same?

There is a pattern in software design that is accepted as the foundation of good practice. It is called MVC (Model, View, Controller). Model is content. View is presentation. Controller is logic.

The application is designed to have something like a database to hold the data content. It has a set of user friendly screens to represent the presentation. It has a set of processing rules to represent the business logic.

These are kept separate to allow any to change without all having to change. If you look closely at a well designed system you will see that each of these parts of the system has its own model, view and controller. Look more closely and you will see that each of these in turn has its own model, view and controller. This continues, in a fractal self similar fashion as far down as you can see.

Fractal Turtles:

In Stephen Hawking's "Brief History Of Time" he tells a story of a scientist, it may have been Bertrand Russell, who was explaining cosmology. He was challenged by a member of his audience who asserted that the world was really a disk on the back of a turtle. The scientist asked the challenger what held the Turtle up. He was answered that it was "Turtles all the way down".

Terry Pratchett's "Discworld" series is based humorously in a world travelling on the back of such a turtle. "Turtles all the way down" is the title of a book written by John Grinder who is one of the originators of NLP along with Richard Bandler.

Apart from the basic interconnectedness of all this, it has caused much talk of infinite regression, prime movers and starting points in philosophical circles.

People can be understood in a similar way. We have our content in our beliefs, values, experience and knowledge. We have our presentation to the world in the way we communicate. We have and our logic in our internal processes, strategies and thoughts.

We have our model of the world, how we present that and our internal dialogue that makes it all fit with what we observe[20].

In order to examine the detail, the consequence and the logical conclusion, we must first of all anchor ourselves to logic. We must anchor ourselves to those things we trust to be true. We can deduce, infer, induce and imply. We build upon the logic of giants and the insight of great magi. If we lose sight of their signposts we must get back to them and start again.

---

20 This idea that we all have our own model causes our hold on reality to fractionate and has led philosophers to sit around for years wondering if they exist or not. Descartes decided that the answer was that if he was asking the question that at least his mind existed. He was not at all sure about anyone else or the physical world.

If what you are doing does not seem to be working, go back to first principles that you trust and examine your application of them.

Remember that if you go too far with any logical argument, if it is not informed, it can lead you down a rabbit hole and lose you. Even the metaphor of existence can appear to fall apart under the scrutiny of incomplete, uninformed logic.

Dark ages rise and fall in the workplace just as they do in life. Tribes form to wage great battles over trivia. They descend into the ignorance of detail. They insist that one instance is proof or that deliberate lack of context is disproof.

One swallow does not a summer make. Did Newton dissect the apple to see what made it fall? Did the inventor of the wheel request a peer review for each wheel? Often when the principles have been misapplied people try to attack the first principles rather than the application.

In all human endeavours, there are general rules that cover generalities, there are specific rules that cover particular circumstances and then there is the study of minutiae. It is essential to know which is which. There are things we take for granted because they have been proven. There are also opinions which are derived from commonly held beliefs which have been mistaken for fact. There is a great difference between opinion and observation.

Opinions must be challenged while observations must be explored.

Principles

It is a very valuable skill to be able to differentiate between opinion and observation, particularly in ourselves.

We need some sort of filter to determine which rules we can trust and which are wolves in sheep's clothing. We need to know which are principles. We need these principles as something against which we can measure possible courses of action.

We need absolute benchmarks like the ancient mariners needed the North star. Otherwise we are led off course and stranded. We can be surrounded by maps and charts but they are useless if they contain no mention of the island we are on.

If we were to do a worldwide poll on what is the most universal principle it is likely it would be the ethic of reciprocity. You may know it as *"Do unto others as you would wish them to do unto you"*.

Many consider it to be the cornerstone of morality and civilisation. It is common to almost all moral codes. It puts you in the other person's shoes so that you consider what they want and what is good for them, even if that is not what you want or what is good for you.

The ancient Greeks expressed it around 600 BC as *"Do not to your neighbour what you would take ill from him."* [21] It has survived almost three thousand years.

The same fellow that said that also said: *"Whatever you do, do it well"* and: *"Forbear to speak evil not only of your friends, but also of your enemies."*

---

21 Pittacus 640-568 BC

So how do we know that a rule is a principle? To draw up some rules for recognising good rules let's have a look at some of the principles that most of us agree on. What are the attributes of a these principles? Here's a suggestion[22].

✔ It is very general.
✔ It is internally consistent.
✔ It can be expressed in the negative and the positive.
✔ It can apply in all situations.
✔ It can be scaled up or down.
✔ It is applicable to everyone.
✔ It is in some way repeatable.
✔ We can derive other working rules from it.
✔ It has stood the test of time and has been tried successfully.
✔ If everyone else applied it, the world would be a nicer place.

You shall not kill

Let's examine this against our criteria:

Is it general?
Yes. It does not talk about any specific type of killing with exceptions or provisos.

Is it internally consistent?
Yes. If it were universally obeyed you would be protected too.

Can it be expressed in the negative and the positive?
You shall preserve life.

Can it apply in all situations?
Whether you agree or not it is applicable everywhere in every culture.

---

22 I am sure there are things that can be added or removed but this is as good a list as any to get us started thinking about it.

Can it be scaled up and down?
You shall not kill this fly. You shall not commit genocide.

Is it applicable to everyone?
"You" means everyone.

Is it repeatable?
It is pretty foolproof.

Can we derive other working rules from it?
If you can't kill directly, you can't kill indirectly and that leads to a lot of rules. You should not smoke over babies. You should drive carefully. You should shout before you hit your golf ball.

Has it stood the test of time and has it been tried successfully?
Our society pretty much hinges on the fact that you are not free to kill people you don't like or whose possessions or jobs you want. We punish people who do.

If everyone else applied it would the world be a nicer place for us to be?
Putting a stop to direct and indirect killing would mean a lot of unpleasantness would go away. It would certainly be a lot nicer to take a walk in certain parts of town.

You can also apply this test to things as diverse as the Model, View, Controller pattern in software development and tightrope walking. What is more, it can get quite abstract. Most of us consider the ability to love to be among the most attractive and worthwhile human endeavours. Before we move on, let us have a look at this description of what many of us might imagine the rules to identifying love to be:

Love is patient, love is kind. It does not envy, it does not boast, it is not proud.
It is not rude, it is not self-seeking, it is not easily angered, it keeps no record of wrongs.
Love does not delight in evil but rejoices with the truth.
It always protects, always trusts, always hopes, always perseveres.[23]

This is recognised by many people, regardless of metaphysical persuasion, as being an accurate guide to recognising love. It appears to comply with the benchmarks that we have set ourselves above.

Can you imagine what it would be like to work with people who fit this description? Would you like your colleagues to describe you like this?

An effective colleague is patient and kind.
An effective colleague does not envy nor boast and is not [arrogant].
An effective colleague is not rude, self-seeking or easily angered.
An effective colleague keeps no record of wrongs.
An effective colleague does not delight in evil but rejoices with the truth.
An effective colleague always protects, always trusts, always hopes, always perseveres.

You may say that this would be all very well if we lived in an ideal world, but all the most professional people I know behave like this.

---

23 4 Corinthians 7

Effective or just efficient

As we traverse our lives we pick up baggage. Some of it is just dead weight and some of it is treasure. We learn to differentiate between efficient and effective.[24] We grow to know that it is possible to be ineffective very efficiently. Recognising this makes all the difference and is the beginning of efficient effectiveness.

We want to change but how can we be sure that we do not throw out the baby with the bathwater? How can we be sure that we do not become the unwitting casualties of tribalism and new ritual? How do we save what was good of the old and how do we avoid the rubbish in the new?

Our society is made up of hyperbole. You just know that the new body spray is more likely to repel than attract the opposite sex, your bank will not give you money for nothing, the kitchen will not gleam and the air freshener will not transport you to a forest glade.

Much of the sales and marketing we are exposed to is designed to make promises based on the need to sell rather than our need for the product. We are surrounded by competition and desperate clawing for the top. We are rats in an experiment. We distrust everyone and miss the things we should trust.

In the midst of all this we have one life, a chance to be amazing. If we chase happiness we will always be chasing it. Tomorrow never comes.

Well, what if you could choose? What if you could become

---

24 Bizarrely the French only have "efficient" to mean both efficient and effective. In the Agile community they borrow the English "effective" and pronounce it as a French word.

your own barometer and true north? What if you could find a way to be an effective judge of value and worth?

Doing and being

I like to think of the people in my life that have really succeeded. It was what they did and the way that they did it that made them who they were. It is who they were that defined what they would do. They acted decisively.

This paradox is the one we must solve. If who we are defines our actions and our actions make us who we are, where do we enter the circle? Like a gear that must attain equivalent velocity before engaging, we must be in order to become. We must become in order to be. Luckily we have people who are willing to tell us how they did it. There is great deal of information available.

What I am going to give you over the following pages is a map that works. In NLP[25] you are continually exhorted to remember that the map is not the territory. This is extremely good advice.

One of the interesting and well meaning myths of the 20th century, and now of the 21st century, is that we are all the same. The other one is that we are all different. We are neither all the same nor is there that much difference between us.

Scale

If you do anything in life that requires you to organise resources to achieve an outcome, then you are a project manager.

Learn to handle scale. When one learns to sing, among the

---

25 See key in next chapter for definition of NLP etc.

first skills to learn is how to find the note deep in your throat, and, once you have found it, to push it out and add volume.

Find something that works then just add scale. First you must learn how to recognise a true note. Once you have it, you sing it out loud and confidently. It is easier to correct it at a low volume than it is to recover from a bellow at full volume. The same applies to what we do at work and in life.

Whatever it is you intend to do, learn to do it honestly and with truth. Honesty and truth scale up. You will know it is true if it really does scale up and retain its shape. Foolishness and erroneous thinking also scale up and become obvious distortions as they inflate. Mostly you will know if something is true when it can expand and change and still remain internally consistent.

Roman or Greek

It is obvious that we need rules, empiricism[26], rigour and repeatability in business and in life. These things save us from repeatedly falling backwards and losing ground to nonsense.

We also need creativity, inspiration, wonder and motivation to ensure that we keep moving forward. While moving forward it is necessary to make sure that the rules are not stifling these more fragile skills. You will notice that anybody who has made a difference, understood the process, but also had the ability to think outside the process.

There is this: There are tools we have been given by our great parents and the minds that went before us. They told us how they reasoned these tools out of nothing and tested them in the flames of intolerance. These are things which we must keep sight of.

---

26 Knowledge based on evidence and experience.

As a civilisation we can begin to recognise that genius takes different forms and has many definitions. It does not always make itself known by great powers of persuasion.

We may find ourselves like that Roman soldier, swinging swords of seniority, wealth, politics, ignorance or status to sever the head of hope, genius, happiness and productivity. Are we yet civilised enough to realise that the power to do something does not give us the right to do it? Will that knowledge be enough to stay our hand?

"I have been thinking," said Arthur, "about Might and Right. I don't think things ought to be done because you are able to do them. I think they should be done because you ought to do them......Might is not right. But there is a lot of Might knocking about in this world, and something has to be done about it..........Why can't you harness Might so that it works for Right? I know it sounds nonsense, but, I mean, you can't just say there is no such thing. The Might is there, in the bad half of people, and you can't neglect it. You can't cut it out but you might be able to direct it, if you see what I mean, so that it was useful instead of bad."
The Once and Future King
- T.H. White

The Key

"If a man empties his purse into his head,
no man can take it away from him.
An investment in knowledge
always pays the best interest."
Benjamin Franklin

Agile

This is an umbrella term for a group of software development methodologies. They are primarily iterative, evolutionary and incremental in nature. They emphasise the importance of communication, innovation, focus on outcome and responding to change.

The Agile manifesto[27] :
✓ *Individuals and interactions over processes and tools.*
✓ *Working software over comprehensive documentation.*
✓ *Customer collaboration over contract negotiation.*
✓ *Responding to change over following a plan.*

They are different to a traditional process driven approach, in that they rely on skilled practitioners who will use experience and teamwork in place of detailed instructions.

TOC – The theory of constraints

This is a set of problem solving thought-tools based on the work of Eli Goldratt. This is a subject worth being familiar with and I strongly recommend you to purchase some of Eli Goldratt's books or recordings. He views a system as a set of interconnections and then uses this insight effectively.

The idea is that when management promotes local optimisations (see the explanation on the following pages) it damages the system as a whole by concentrating on local throughputs rather than the flow of the system as a whole.

---

27 http://agilemanifesto.org/

TOC concentrates on finding the constraint that is affecting the whole system. It is similar in some ways to critical path analysis in that you look at the flow from beginning to end.

It deals with the idea of very complex systems. It promotes the idea of following the critical constraint as it moves from place to place in the system. It advocates managing it to acceptable levels from the point of view of the goal of the system. The emphasis is on understanding the effect of change on the system as a whole.

This thinking is very much informed by Systems Thinking. The advice is to identify the constraints in any system and to avoid local optimisations. Problems are seen as undesired effects of an underlying cause and they can be used as clues to find it.

The concept of Local Optimisations is worth explaining here:

A local optimisation is an optimisation that optimises the efficiency of only part of the system. In many cases this has either no effect or a detrimental effect on the system as a whole.

Consider the effect of adding many lanes and kiosks on a motorway just before a toll bridge that has only two lanes. The road leading up to the toll bridge may seem to be taking more cars and the ability to process cars and get them on to the bridge may be more efficient; but this is a local efficiency. The overall throughput does not change. The bridge itself is a bottleneck. It can only take two lanes of traffic no matter how fast the traffic arrives.

We do the same in business. An example would be giving people and teams targets which do not benefit the delivery as a whole.

The example I frequently use to explain this is a hypothetical bicycle factory in which different parts of the bicycle are being made by different departments. We can optimise each department so that it is operating at maximum capacity.

We exhort each department with targets and rewards for increased output.

Say we end up with a daily output of 100 saddles, 400 wheels, 50 frames and 6 gearing mechanisms.

No matter what we do in the other departments we can only make a maximum of 6 complete bikes a day if 6 gears is the maximum output of the gearing department.

All the other wheels, saddles and frames are just cluttering up the factory and tying up our cash-flow in stored inventory.

Systems-thinking says that you find that bottleneck and that this controls the speed of delivery.

This leads you to the startling conclusion that more productivity from the other departments is actually a problem.

You need to find a way to produce more of whatever is

holding everything else up, if this is the constraint. In this case you look at what it would take to produce more gears.

↑Design simpler gears
☛ Introduce more automation
☛ Add a second gearing department
↑Is there a local bottleneck in the gearing department itself?
☛ Are they waiting on materials or parts?
☛ How are they assembling and testing the gears?
☛ Can the gears be delivered to bicycle assembly istages?
☛ Does the gearing department need to be split into different functional departments?
☛ Does it need to have closer ties with another department?

We still need to be aware of the WHOLE system. If you can only sell 5 bicycles a day then Sales is the bottleneck not the production of gears. Until you can sell 6 or more bicycles a day, we are overproducing gears.

We must follow the bottleneck as it moves. Any optimisation must speed up the system as a whole or it is just a local optimisation with no benefit.

Systems Thinking

The basis of Systems Thinking is that every system is part of a bigger system and that no system is completely isolated. It appears to challenge the idea of reductionism. It has been embraced by thought leaders from Charles Darwin to Gregory Bateson.

Everything can be considered as a system. Every system is part of a larger system. Your job is part of your department, your department is part of your company, your company is part of a business sector, that sector is part of the economy of the country, the economy of the country is part of the world economy, world economy is part of human civilisation, which is part of life on this planet which is part of existence in the universe.

In short you need to be aware of what the marketing plans for your company are before you make radical changes to your product. Marketing people tend to be quite proficient at Systems Thinking because they need to know all about trends, cause and effect and the behaviour of the market as a whole.

The reality is that to understand whether something is a good idea or not, you need to understand how it relates to the systemic levels all around you. This chunking up, down and sideways is a big part of the thinking of the rest of this book. I will sometimes refer to it as hierarchy, context or scope for the benefit of developers who find their way in here.

Lateral Thinking

Edward De Bono is famously associated with this type of approach. It offers an alternative to the traditional method of problem solving which delves into the detail. Instead, lateral thinking seeks to move sideways and take advantage of existing possibilities. It does this by moving up the hierarchy, across and then down again.

E.g. my car is broken down so I can't get to town. Is my problem one of fixing my car? No. What is the car one of? A method of transport (up). What are other methods of transport (across and back down)? I could walk, get the bus, get a lift with my friend, roller skate, cycle or go by train. I decide to cycle because it preserves my independence. The net effect is of a lateral, or sideways, move.

NLP – Neuro Linguistic Programming

This is based primarily on the work of Richard Bandler and John Grinder. It is concerned with the way we interface with the world around us and the way we represent it to ourselves.

NLP provides a number of tools that enable us to understand our own internal strategies, control them and model the strategies of the people we admire and wish to emulate. It also provides ways to appreciate that other models of the world exist and makes suggestions as to how to communicate across these models.

Metaphor and the unconscious mind

In one sense everything is a metaphor. Words are metaphors for meanings. Images are light metaphors. Sounds are noise metaphors. Language is a metaphor for understanding. What we see, and how our brain interprets it, is a metaphor for what may really be there.

There are two sides to what we call ourselves. There is the conscious part that is like a driver and the unconscious part that is made up of the experiences, habits, interpretations, wishes, wants, beliefs and values.

Imagine a big spreadsheet. At any one time you can only see a fraction of the whole thing on your computer. You can focus on only a single screen-full at a time. That is your conscious mind. The rest of the spreadsheet is still there carrying out all the things you told it to. All the calculations you programmed into the cells are reacting to new inputs. It is working away not quite in the background but not quite in the foreground. That is your unconscious mind.

Your unconscious mind loves images, symbols and metaphors. It takes language literally, which can be dangerous because it does not understand negatives - so I won't tell you to not worry about it.

That last sentence is difficult because there are negatives in it.

If I say to you to not think of an orange, your brain has to think of an orange because you are parsing the language in order to identify what you need to do with it.

The information about the orange is then passed to the logical part of your mind, to show it what not to think about.

If it makes it easier you can think of your right brain[28] as the bit of you that deals with symbols and metaphors. It hears "do blank think blank orange". It identifies the things and actions and then it passes the lot to the left brain which knows what to do with "not" and the "of".

If it helps you, think of "Not" as a logical function and your left brain as the bit that deals with logical functions. It gets "item:Orange; action:think; logical function:not". It then goes into a sort of processing loop.

---

28 It is better to think of the left brain, right brain split as a metaphor. Although there is evidence that there are tendencies for the right hemisphere to focus on big picture and the left hemisphere to focus on detail, neuroscientists tell us it is more subtle than that. For instance, in his book "The Brain that Changes Itself", Norman Diodge presents lots of evidence that the brain is not as hard-wired as previously thought and that it is a great deal more flexible.

Yep – got the orange, shiny round thing with a nice taste when ripe, waxy pitted peel and associated with vitamin C, juggling and breakfast drinks. I know how to think, imagine, want, desire, worry, describe, picture. Now apply "not". Okay stop thinking about oranges. Access oranges. Yep that's what I am not thinking about: oranges. Memo to self not to think about oranges. What are they? Yes, there they are, the oranges I am not thinking about. What am I not thinking about? Oh yes, oranges.

If I say "Think of an apple" you are fine. You thought of an apple and the job's done.

Now if I say "Do not, not think of oranges!".
Did you feel the internal stutter?

Happily the unconscious mind decodes metaphor just fine. Much better than your conscious in fact. This could explain why all civilizations ever discovered have some form of poetry and some form of story telling.

We all love stories. If you can remember that teacher you loved, I bet they were great at the language of metaphor. Children love to learn in stories. Great teachers and philosophers use stories to communicate complex ideas.

Metaphor attempts to see through the surface structure of language to the deep structure of meaning. It bypasses the pointer, if you like, and gets straight to the value being pointed at - by showing you something equivalent.

Unlike a direct explanation, a metaphor does not pretend to be the real thing. When we do not use metaphor and instead use the direct language of rationality, there is a clash of values as two things try to occupy the same space.

At its best, metaphor is a communication tool. It finds a common level of understanding and anchors the current reality to it.

If I give you a metaphor I am inviting you to temporarily let go of your usual way of looking at something and I am prepared to let go of mine. Metaphor is like walking together on a mutually unusual path.

We all have routines. Have you ever got into your car to go to the shops on Saturday and found yourself accidentally on the way to work?

Metaphor is a way of reminding ourselves of the destination and of making sure we do not slip into a well worn rut just because it is there.

Metaphor invites you to take a different perspective and thereby look more critically at what is going on.

Refinement versus reductionism

Reductionism is a process of breaking things down to their component parts. Reductionists attempt to understand something by taking it apart and looking at how each of the pieces work at their most atomic level and in their interactions with each other.

Of course there are benefits from peeling back layers and examining something step by step. Much of science is based on this approach.

The danger is that one can miss the interactions and patterns in the system as a whole if one is not aware of the significance of the information being revealed; or if one skips layers in an attempt to over simplify.

Many systems in nature, science, philosophy and life, increasingly appear to be more than the sum of their parts as we discover more about them.

Take a piece of complex classical music, a symphony perhaps. If you were to listen to each instrument in isolation, you would probably find the music uninspiring. You would probably end up with very little notion about how the symphony works or how it sounds as a full entity. It would be difficult to isolate what is essential.

In schenkerian analysis of music, however, a piece is reduced to its simplest form with a purpose. It is a way to look beneath the surface and identify the underlying shapes and patterns that span the piece and explore the music beyond the surface notes.

Music is a hierarchy of layers and, depending on which layer you are in, there are relationships of varying scope.

The more you reduce or simplify the music, the more these relationships become apparent. In this sort of reductionism the objective is to find the most basic form of the music, identify the relationships within the piece and understand the complexities by comparing them to the simplest form.

What I refer to disparagingly as "reductionist nonsense" is the sort of reductionism which seeks to isolate and compartmentalise. It is a mechanistic and arrogant reductionism that allows no room for discovery or change. I am talking about the sort of reductionism in management, design and living that seeks to ignore the dependencies between things. It seeks to control through a policy of divide and conquer.

It is the sort of reductionism that seeks to replace skill with process. It seeks to replace judgement with rules. It seeks to put people in boxes and refuses to let them grow.

Refinement, on the other hand, is the process of identifying the essential ingredients that make something work and of discarding the unnecessary. It is a continuous process.

In NLP this is called modelling. Good modellers know that it is not just how a person stands, moves or talks that makes a master.

Merely reducing a great athlete, a great chef or a great musician down to their external actions will give you valuable information but not enough to really understand why what they are doing is great. You need to understand how they are thinking, their internal dialogue and how value judgements are calibrated for that. You need to start understanding their map of the world on their terms. You need to unravel the layers.

Most importantly you need to understand how these things interact and whether or not there are synaesthesia[29]. You need to know this in order to know what is necessary. To take away what is not necessary you need to understand and appreciate what is necessary. There is always more going on than is apparent.

It is not what they are doing but how.

---

29 A cross wiring of the senses. Sounds can be seen, smells can be felt etc. People can use these synaesthesia in how they think about and achieve things. For example a musician who associates colours with sounds may have a unique way of composing and playing associated with this.

Following a recipe might give you good results under the same circumstances that the recipe was taken. If something is different you need to first of all know that it is different and secondly be able to adjust what you are doing to take account of it. In other words you need a reasonably deep understanding of the first principles even to follow a recipe.

In software development it is why Artificial Intelligence is so long coming. Language is not just a matter of words and meanings. It also requires understanding of nuance, subtlety, tone, context, social norms, cultural references and reading refinements in humour, mood and body language.

In order to refine something you need to understand the interactions and the subtleties of it. You need to understand relative priorities and the fuzzy logic of it. You need to understand how relationships span the whole.

Alistair Cockburn was the first I heard talking about Shu Ha Ri in his book[30]. It is a concept from Japanese martial arts. It is about learning something to mastery. People who learn Akido will be familiar with it. It is a meta rule like "model view controller" and "doing unto others".

Shu – (protect or obey) You learn and follow the rules.
Ha – (detach or digress) You find the limits of the rules.
Ri – (leave or separate) You can do it without the rules.

Mastery is when it has become natural. It is now part of who you are. It is in the muscle.

The Chinese have a similar concept which is Ti Ren Tian.

---

30 Agile Software Development by Alistair Cockburn.

Ti – (Earth) You know the basics.
Ren – (Human) You are ready to learn.
Tian – (Heaven) There is no conscious thought in doing it.

In the West we are more likely to know it as the route from unconscious incompetence to unconscious competence.

Unconscious incompetence
– You do not know that you are incompetent at something.
Conscious incompetence
– You become aware that you are incompetent at something.
Conscious competence
 – You know the rules and you have to concentrate on doing it competently.
Unconscious competence
– You do it right without thinking about it.

If you have ever learned to play a musical instrument you will have gone through these stages. If you ever learned to play a sport you will have gone through these stages.

You may have had a few lessons from a friend and you think you are doing great. Then you take a lesson from a professional or you learn enough to start to appreciate what real playing is all about.

The same goes for driving, programming, using a sledgehammer, learning a language or juggling.

What you will notice as you learn something - or even talk to the greatest expert you can find - is that these stages are not one off, one time, stages. As you progress you find that there are levels of mastery.

As you reach unconscious competence on one level you are only happy there for a while before you realise you are unconsciously incompetent at the next level. The next level may not even be one you had been aware existed.

Think of the person who is so far ahead at something that you feel you would need several lifetimes to catch up with them. If you were to talk to them and they are a true master they will still be going through this process. Each level brings a new challenge and you can see more possibilities and levels ahead.

Ask any scientific researcher and they will tell you that each new discovery or breakthrough asks more questions than it answers.

Learning looks something like this:

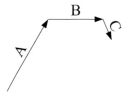

Learning Cycle

A) Learning new skills
B) Plateau as you think you have it mastered
C) Realisation and unlearning as you prepare for the next level

It is recursive and fractal.

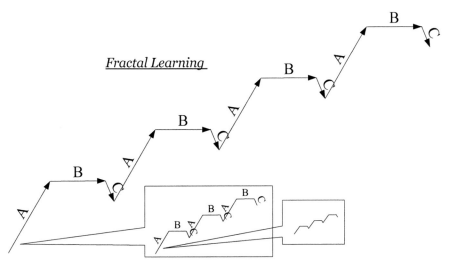

Fractal Learning

Each stage is itself made up of stages.

Think of learning something. You might remember learning to drive a car, to play a musical instrument or perhaps to read and write. Whatever you learn, you will find you need a collection of complimentary skills. If you analyse each of these skills in turn, you will find each one is, itself, made up of a collection of skills. The deeper you analyse the more levels of skill you will find.

At each level you make use of skills you already have and learn new skills. To increase the meta skill at each level you need to go through the process of augmenting or learning the constituent skills.

This has a fortunate side effect, which is that it is impossible to isolate these skills for one task only. As I become a better guitarist I get finer motor control of my fingers, which helps with other things which require manual dexterity.

As we learn things in this fashion we create neural connections and open neural pathways. The more we learn the easier it is to learn. The more you put in your head the more capacity you have. My five year old daughter is fond of telling us that if you use your brains they grow.

You may look at a cubist painting by Picasso and you may be tempted to think that that he knew nothing about the rules of perspective. It was actually his deep knowledge of the rules of perspective that allowed him to break them so spectacularly in an attempt to paint things as they were on the inside.

Patterns

One of the ways we learn is to recognise patterns.

Design patterns are maps left by previous travellers. They are successful recipes. Very good patterns do not give you step by step directions but they do tell you what success looks like. They have markers that tell you what pitfalls to avoid.

The pattern sets down the objective. It lays out the elements and why they are important. It is internally consistent.

A pattern is also a set of things that repeat a relationship. Our brains are outstanding at pattern recognition. Sometimes it is conscious, sometimes unconscious. You will like a piece of music because on an unconscious level you have recognised a mathematical pattern deep in the notes and the rhythm. It pleases you in ways you can only begin to understand.

The Fibonacci sequence of numbers, where each is the product of the two preceding numbers, is a less obvious pattern. It takes your conscious mind a while to get to grips with it but is recognised easily by your unconscious.

The Key

1,1,2,3,5,8,13,21,34,55

The relationship between these numbers (approx 1.618) is considered to be very special by artists, architects, musicians, mathematicians, biologists and psychologists. It occurs everywhere in nature. It is in the ratio of branches on plants, the swirl of a snail shell and the contours of a coastline. It is called phi **Φ** or the golden ratio.

It seems to have been discovered about 400 BC and has fascinated the likes of Leonardo Da Vinci, Johannes Kepler and our own century's mathematicians and theorists such as Roger Penrose[31]. It pops up in geometry with alarming frequency and is considered by some to be a universal rule.

Great works of art and music have been found to be riddled with it consciously and unconsciously.

Mathematics can be considered to be the science of patterns[32].

Fractals are mathematical patterns that are scale invariant. It does not matter how closely you look at them or scale them up or down. They are self similar on any scale of magnification. They reflect natural patterns found on coastlines, plants and biological organisms. Fractal analysis is an important part of modern scientific research.

Rules

Rules are based on patterns. The more universal the pattern, the more universal the rule. Rules are inherited from principles in context. The context of the rule should be understood. Outside that context the rule may or may not

---

31 http://intendo.net/penrose/info.html
32 http://mathdl.maa.org/mathDL/1/?
    pa=content&sa=viewDocument&nodeId=437&bodyId=465

have meaning. Rules that have to work in a variety of contexts need to be flexible.

A principle is a rule that works everywhere. This can be natural - "plants need water to grow"; or by common agreement - "green means go".

Even then we have to be careful. Most of us take nodding to mean yes. There are places in the world where it means no.

Look right before crossing is a great rule in the UK but could get you killed in many other parts of the world.

Just because a rule is correct in one place or time does not make it a rule you can trust. The old saying that "rules are made to be broken" means that you need to question rules all the time to make sure that they are still being entirely honest with you.

Methodology

I find it helps to think of methodology as an attempt to discover rules that work so that we can apply them elsewhere.

Too many methodologies exist to solely benefit the vendors, the tribe that claims it as theirs, the career of methodologists or the control freak that has sneaked on to our project undetected.

I am proposing that we reclaim methodology as a tool we can sharpen for ourselves and apply to the job at hand.

Creativity

Some managers, when confronted with this word, start to zip up their purses. It conjures up images of castles in the air, white elephants, over engineered solutions and avoidable waste. I think that they may have it too tightly bound to the word accounting and that they suppose that the last thing they want is expensive genius, when they could have some well behaved process followers.

Some years ago I started working for a company that was having a number of problems with its IT department. There was a project that was stuck and had been stuck for many months.

My job was to look at what was sticking it. I discovered that they were waiting for a generic solution for the part of the program whose job it was to load data into a central system. They were bringing in a large company to analyse and code a solution with a projected lead time of another 6 months.

I had a look at the code. I found that the problem was that the data was not in standard arrays but in bitmaps[33]. Each bitmap had a different format. The standard coding practice, iterating over the array, could not cope with this.

I wrote a program which included a separate module to load each bitmap rather than one module capable of loading all the bitmaps. There were only twenty five.

The argument against doing this was that the code would have to be changed with every change to the bitmaps. My reason for doing it this way was that I had looked at the change history and I had observed that there had been only

---

33 Digital information is held in bits which can be either one or zero. On computers these bits are arranged into arrays of eight bits or multiples of eight. Computer languages can be told to examine the next bit or the next multiple of eight bits. Bitmaps were used when memory was at a premium and allowed the program to hold data in any multiple of bits. You need to know how the information is mapped in order to retrieve it.

one bitmap changed since the system had been installed.

In the end I had written the program in a maintainable fashion in less than a week. I estimated that a total bitmap change would take less than a day to make and test.

The cost of writing the code was 1/52 of my salary and the solution was more robust and less error prone than a complex outsourced solution.

My creativity had saved the company at least 6 months, thousands of pounds of development and a costly maintenance contract. It did not involve anything costly or particularly exotic.

The key ingredient was the particular IT manager's positive attitude to creativity. He encouraged and supported me. It does not surprise me to find that he is now a respected industry leader who is much in demand.

Creative solutions are the goal of the responsible manager who is not just paying lip service to the "work smarter, not harder" maxim.

Intent

- Where to look
- How to look
- What to look for
- How to know when you have found it

Turning the key

NLP allows you to challenge your perceptions and to begin to understand the perceptions of others. It allows you to identify beliefs. It allows you determine if those beliefs are aiding or restraining you.

Systems-thinking allows you to change perspective and stand outside your assumptions. It allows you to see the foundations and what is supporting those foundations. It allows you to see what is really affecting you. It allows you to define the big picture of your current reality.

The Theory of Constraints allows you to examine cause and effect. It gives you tools to work your way out of your assumptions and constraints. It allows you to get things in perspective and to inform your focus.

Agile thinking allows you to accept chaos and to take advantage of change. It helps you to deal with changing perceptions and accept that outcomes change. It provides some basic tools to deal with time, cost, ability, collaboration and progress.

These are not the only tools. There are other tools like them. Use them but remember that they are but tools. You should ensure that you prevent them from becoming constraints. Keep your eyes, ears and mind open for new tools. They are constantly being developed.

Order is temporary. Chaos is the natural state. This is the principle of entropy. Entropy is a measure of work to be done; and like a coiled spring it must unfold. Everything that exists is energy waiting to be released. Order is work to be done. Stability is an illusion – from the moment we build our castles they begin to decay.

Entropy is a landslide and our glory is the dance we do on top of it.

Inspiration

"If I have seen farther than others, it is because I was standing on the shoulders of giants."
Sir Isaac Newton

Inspiration for a change

Have you ever been inspired? Can you think of a time when you watched someone doing something, heard them saying something, felt the passion they communicated or just found that their skill had transported you? Maybe it was an actor in a film, a musician, an artist, a writer. Maybe it was a colleague or a friend. Maybe it was a complete stranger. Maybe it was all of the above and more.

I have been inspired so many times in my life that I have lost count. The word inspired suggests to me the act of breathing in, the breathing in of another's spirit. Lately I hear a song or read a book and almost feel that I have taken part in that act of creation myself. I feel a deep and profound love of that person who had the spark to communicate that piece of their understanding of it all to me.

Some of these have been people in my own life that I can see, hear and touch in front of me. Sometimes it has been through the recordings they made of their insights. The ability to inspire is one of the greatest. For me it is the reason behind the reason for art, community, friendship, love and getting up in the morning.

I have yet to meet a person who has never been inspired by somebody else, whether it was a great leader like Julius Caesar or Robert Kennedy, a man of great humanity like Gandhi or Martin Luther King, Jr. or a "virtuoso" in some field like Einstein, Shakespeare, Mohammed Ali, Louis Armstrong or Neil Armstrong.

So whatever else I think I know, I am sure that you and I have this experience in common. We have at some time, at least once, been inspired by another human being.

The meaning of life

In 2004 I was taking a sabbatical to renovate a house in France and to renovate my thinking. We had no TV and life went gloriously back to basics. The stresses of work and, to some extent, the 21st century began to drain from my mind.

When we got a phone line installed we registered for a dial up internet connection. We started reading the papers online. The news was shocking, the USA had invaded Iraq in 2003 and the inconsistencies in British and US policies were becoming apparent.

We sat at the kitchen table late into the evening when the kids had gone to bed and we talked about it. We felt that the world outside our corner of France was becoming very dark indeed.

Then in September 2004 I used the same internet connection to read an article by Julian Baggini[34] about the meaning of life[35].

He talked about the occasion when Bertrand Russell[36] was asked by a cabbie in London what it was all about, life and

---

34 Editor of the Philosophers Magazine but according to his website a lot more http://julianbaggini.blogspot.com/
35 http://www.guardian.co.uk/theguardian/2004/sep/20/features11.g2
36 Bertrand Russell (1872-1970): Philosopher, mathematician, historian, advocate for social reform and pacifist. He was outspoken against totalitarianism; he criticized Hitler, the Soviet Union and America's involvement in Vietnam. He was a humanitarian and a champion of free thought. He urged Nuclear Disarmament. With Whitehead he wrote Principia Mathematica of which you will later be hearing much more.

such. Russell hesitated to answer. What stopped him, claims Baggini, were the presuppositions in the question.

There are presuppositions that there is a meaning to life, that someone ordained that meaning, that this meaning was a purpose and furthermore, that the purpose would make sense.

In the article Baggini gives an answer by asking why the cabbie had asked the question and by asking what the cabbie might have actually wanted to know.

He suggests that a question from Camus[37] might be the question really being asked. The question is not what is the meaning of life but rather why shouldn't we kill ourselves? Why should we think that this life, with all its problems and pressures is valuable in itself?

He is then able to give the answer given by Woody Allen's character in the film Manhattan *"Groucho Marx; Willie Mays; the second movement of the Jupiter Symphony; Louis Armstrong's recording of Potato-head Blues; Swedish movies; Sentimental Education by Flaubert; Marlon Brando; Frank Sinatra; those incredible apples and pears by Cézanne; the crabs at Sam Wo's"*. He suggests that we all have our own lists and that they constitute the answer to the meaning of our life.

---

37 Albert Camus (1913-60): Philosopher. His works focus on the positive side of Surrealism and Existentialism and reject the Nihilism of others such as Jean Paul Sartre. He opposed totalitarianism, particularly that of Hitler and later the Soviet Union.

Recursion and the main narrative

The recursive nature of this experience startled me:

> I was inspired by somebody
> who was inspired by many
> inspired people
> and by the experiences
> that inspired them
> and him
> and me.

There is a lot to be enjoyed in life if we stop wasting time stressing about the small stuff and get on with the main narrative. In the always inspirational words of John Lennon in a song he wrote for his son *"**Life is what happens to you while you are busy making other plans"***.

People can be knocked off the main narrative for years. I remember a sobering moment in the office many years ago as I worked late. I glanced at a colleague's vacant desk and saw that he had pinned a note under a photo of his children "At the end, no one wishes they had spent more time in the office".

The title of this volume is "Working Life". If you offer people a life that works and includes the things they care about; if it includes those things on the list that gives their life meaning, they will be inspired.

If people are motivated it means they do something because of some projected pay-off. If that pay-off does not arrive it is going to be harder to motivate them the next time. If you start down this track with people, you have to maintain it and you may not always have the motivations to offer.

If people are inspired, they do the work because they enjoy it and find meaning in doing it well.

If work fits into that list of things that gives life meaning then people start to find happiness in the way they do things. This leads to a massive increase in productivity and quality. This is dealt with explicitly in volume two under the heading of happiness.

There are two things we have in common:
> We have been inspired.
> Somewhere, tucked away, we have a list of things that make our life worth living.

I find in my life that the longer I make the list, the easier it is to get up in the morning.

This morning I got up already thinking about the people in my life who inspire me and why it happens that they do. What is it about these people that makes them leaders, teachers, mentors, coaches and people to whom I listen? Why do I listen to them even when I find their statements challenging? What is it that makes some people the inspiration of us all?

Exploring this is central to what I am asking you to consider and it is important that I make this clear as we set off. You should have some idea where we are headed. Maybe you will even arrive there before me.

Thought renovation

There are some ideas that seem to be outside time, space and circumstance. They are abstract ideas that can manifest themselves practically in any set of circumstances. The more circumstances in which something is true, the more interesting it becomes.

The Tao Te Ching[38] for instance, is an ancient Chinese text. At first it may seem a little strange to introduce this. What possible relevance could it have?

There are two things we are going to consider.

The first is an interesting idea the writer introduces. It is that anyone who thinks that they understand the Tao clearly does not. It is not about understanding it is about being.

As a programmer this makes sense, although I am careful not to claim I understand it. Recursion is a valuable tool to developers. I have heard it referred to as the dragon that eats its tail.

Recursion is an idea that uses itself. Like two mirrors facing each other, the image is recursive. In programming it is a function that calls itself. You normally get out of a recursion when some defined condition has been met.

For instance a simple recursive function would be one which adds a number to a total and calls itself again or exits based on a total.

- I am passed a running total and a target
- I add one to the total
- If the total is less than the target I call myself again and I inform myself of the running total and the target

---

38 http://academic.brooklyn.cuny.edu/core9/phalsall/texts/taote-v3.html or http://www.chinapage.com/gnl.html. The version I first read was the translation by Richard Wilhelm. Like many of these things there is some academic infighting about what represents the proper translation but if you read a couple of translations you start to get the general idea.

• Otherwise I print out the total and stop

The second is the idea of being the un-carved block. Being full of possibility. Being able to accept that which is, with equanimity. Being ready for the future with an open mind.

Unpacking change

I like to explain things by putting them into words in certain way. I want the words to be words that allow me to keep thinking about whatever it is I am explaining.

I have found that giving people definitive answers does not help them. If I give them packed information, clues and strategies for thinking, they tend to be happier and more self sufficient when I visit them to see how things are going.

Then there are things that I like to leave open ended for further learning and change, no matter how well they seem to have been absorbed.

Milton H. Ericsson was one of the people whose work was modelled to create NLP. He was a master of inspiration. He was a master of language. If he were to want you to think of something relaxing, he would ask you to imagine your most relaxing experience. If he wanted he could address multitudes and they would all imagine a relaxing experience.

If he had tried to describe his own most relaxing experience it would only have worked for some. The sort of language he did use, encouraged people to connect with their own deep structure.

A key to inspiring is to use this example. People who are not good leaders limit success to their own vision. People who are great leaders expand their definition of success to encompass the dreams of their colleagues. They inspire them to find their own answers and draw their own conclusions.

Consider John F Kennedy's inaugural speech simply as an example of this. "Ask not what your country can do for you but what you can do for your country". That meant something different to everyone who heard it. He told no one what to do. At the same time he created an imperative that was difficult to argue with.

In the same era Martin Luther King, Jr. said he had a dream of freedom. His dream was inclusive. As you read or listen to his speech, as it soars towards a climax of a dream of freedom for former slaves; former slave owners and finally, all of humanity, you realise it is only bounded by what you can choose to dream is possible.

Inspirational leaders and teachers all do this one thing, they refuse to restrict a finishing post or an acceptable level of achievement. They harness the best in people and the best that people can imagine. They describe the dreams of others by unfettering their own.

If you think I am talking about being vague, read these two speeches and notice the precision with which this is done. Their words and ideas unpack in the ear and mind of the listener.

Some teachers can give you compressed information in a way that unpacks as you think about it and apply it to your own experience. It is more flexible than a list of situations, their problems and their solutions.

Jonathan Haidt talks about the happiness hypotheses and quotes Stephen Pinker. He has two ideas that are interesting here and which give us a clue as to why and how this works.

The first is that real change only comes about by degrees[39]. Regardless of our intent and determination, we are all riding an elephant called habit. It has to be trained to turn by small feedback loops. It does not respond to screaming, shouting, violence or good intentions. Left to its own devices it will follow its habits.

The second is that, regardless of where or when we are in the world, it seems that we are all born with certain moral values in common[40]. I will list them here and discuss them again later.

The five values are

- Harm/Care
- Fairness/Reciprocity
- In group/loyalty
- Authority/Respect
- Purity/Sanctity

Imagine leadership that is based on the understanding that these things are subjective and that they are genetically hard wired.

People respond instinctively away from harm and towards care. People respond positively to fairness and display reciprocity. People naturally like to belong to a group and will exhibit loyalty. We recognise authority and we seek respect. We value the pure and we have things we hold dear.

---

39 http://www.happinesshypothesis.com/
40 http://www.ted.com/index.php/talks/jonathan_haidt_on_the_moral_mind.html

Belief in context

In a talk with a good friend the other night, after a couple of glasses of wine, he made the statement that acceptance is the opposite of belief. This took a bit of thinking about but we boiled it down to this:

Belief is an act of will; acceptance is an act of faith.

We have a tendency to confuse them and create wars over this confusion.

Throughout history there is a great deal of evidence that the willingness to die for ones beliefs is considered a virtue. I would contend that the ability to let go of your beliefs is the real virtue. The ability to change with the context is the harder and, ultimately, the more rewarding thing to do.

In any given situation we must be careful not to confuse context with reality. I have a mental image of a group of us in one end of a dark box. We have a little flashlight. We are delighted that we can see what is there at our end and we start declaring our end to be all that exists. The proof we offer is that this end is all we can see.

Now there are two types of people in our group. One type wants to continue to study what can be seen and the other type wants to take the light and have a look at what might be at the other end of the box.

I realise that this metaphor will probably make you start thinking about thinking outside the box. That is exactly right. The box is really an onion and outside this box is another and outside that is another like Russian dolls. Metaphors within metaphors.

Inspiration

In Terry Pratchett's "Sourcery" his characters are in the desert with an old lamp, in which they find a thoroughly modern genie. They ask him to transport them out of the desert to the distant city.

They immediately find themselves bumping along in what seems suspiciously like the inside of a lamp. It turns out that they are inside the lamp which one of them is carrying.

It is a reasonable proposition, it transpires, to be moving. They are inside the lamp which is moving. One of them is carrying the lamp. Because they are moving of course the lamp is moving. If the lamp is moving of course the person carrying the lamp is moving. They have to not think about it in case reality notices and puts a stop to it.[41]

I know it is a bit silly, but this recursive metaphor describes our relationship with reality beautifully. We have to make sense of the immensity and chaos of it so we make boundaries from context. This is a great ability to have. It allows us to adapt and function in almost any situation.

The danger is that this ability to compartmentalise can lead us to forget that we ourselves created the boundaries. We forget that we can and should control these boundaries. When they start controlling us we need to remember that they are just metaphors.

If we forget, we can create beliefs from context and often resist any efforts to then shift the context. We can become convinced that expedient make-believe, such as the financial system, is real. We imprison ourselves in jobs and living rooms, patrolled by supervisors and TV show hosts. We

---

41 Terry Pratchett's books are not only enormously entertaining and clever but they can be educational and greatly inspiring. He is a grand master of metaphor.

imbue the wrong things with too much importance and limit our ways to succeed.

Our intent was pure but the road to hell is paved with good intentions.

One of Shakespeare's most quoted quotes is:
"There are more things in heaven and earth, Horatio,
Than are dreamt of in your philosophy." [42]
This is worth remembering.

Men and women who have listened to this have changed the world. They challenged their own beliefs and the accepted beliefs of their times. They challenged the belief that the world was flat, that the sun orbited the earth, that heavier than air flight was impossible and that only things you could see could affect you.

Sometimes this challenge of belief can appear pointless and you may question the point of walking on the moon. Where is the return on investment on that one? I would say it is magnificent. It pushes the boundaries of what we believe to be possible.

Because of people who chose to be unconstrained by the boundaries of belief, we are learning of the wonders of interstellar space, we can explore our own planet, we have medicines that save lives and we are handed wondrous knowledge about the nature of the universe undreamed of by previous generations - or Horatio.

It could be argued that it was their belief in something that allowed them to achieve these things. It all depends on what you are labelling belief.

---

42 Hamlet Act 1, scene 5, 159-167

Like many words it is overloaded. This belief describes an opening up to the possibilities of what could be and an acceptance of what is.

The belief that constrains us is the belief in absolutes.

A good idea for its time

We live in metaphorical boxes which represent the boundaries that we create. We contextualise in order to deal with things. We cannot deal with all of everything and the constantly changing nature of things so we create islands of permanence. They are metaphors that allow us to operate.

Consider a child growing up. At any given time their own size is an absolute reference to the world around them. Yet over time this absolute is changing. The child has the ability to know, at some level, that they are growing. They unconsciously and constantly reappraise the size of things so that they can pick up that fork and judge the distance to the table.

If you were to live your life constantly aware of your own mortality you would not function because nothing would be important or everything would be too important. So we construct a world in which we are alive and we have boundaries of time: yesterday, today, tomorrow and the next financial quarter. We know these are only absolutes while we maintain that context. Tomorrow becomes today and the absolute now is only true in context of when I am.

Similarly we ascribe absolutes of "right and wrong" and "good and bad" to things, events and perceptions. In itself nothing is good or bad or even right or wrong except in context. In that context it is fair and appropriate to ascribe those attributes.

The danger lies in trying to make universals out of them.

"It seemed like a good idea at the time" is not so much an excuse as a valid explanation of what is always happening to us. The leaders of the revolution become the guardians of the new status quo.

Context in belief

If we have a methodology for managing projects, we do the best we can in the context as we understand it. I am familiar with software development projects so my examples will be in that domain. We examine the issues and information we have about what we are trying to do. We do some things that work. We sensibly record them and develop a process.

Then the context changes. In software development, as in business, society and the affairs of men, the context is always changing. In fact we humans handle "change" really well. It is why we have been so successful as a species. We seem to be able to adapt to almost anything. [43]

If some of us try to hold on to the methodology as the context changes we get conflict. As with the meaning of life, we ask the wrong questions.

We start asking which methodology is the best. We start attacking the old methodology outside of its context, as if it were an absolute. We start measuring how well the new methodology will achieve what the old methodology was trying to achieve; as if that were more important than clarifying what we now need to achieve in the new context. Lines are drawn for attack and defence.

---

[43]Rats are the only other species on the planet as good at adapting as we are and can be found wherever mankind sets down roots; from the icy wastes of the north pole to the furnaces of the hottest deserts.

This is counter productive and I would like to move our focus away from it. Let me explain what is right about what we are doing and what we are trying to do.

Motivation and filters

There are many ways to describe the different sorts of human beings. Dividing them into two camps is the usual way. This is because we seem to be made up of a number of binary attributes. To make it even more confusing there is rarely an absolute setting. There are preferred settings but even they are context dependent.

We can be motivated by fear or desire. We go towards something or away from something. This is sometimes referred to as carrot and stick. Even if we have a preference as to how we are motivated, we can still be motivated by the other.

Are you motivated to get up and go to work in the morning by the fear that you will lose your job and that your family will starve?

Are you motivated to get up and go to work because you are working toward a promotion or a project delivery that will give you more job satisfaction?

Although one is a stick and the other is a carrot many of us would interpret both of these as fairly moral reasons to be motivated. However people with different motivating patterns can clash badly when it comes to beliefs and working together.

For instance people motivated out of fear will be risk averse and people motivated out of desire to succeed will seek out opportunity, which may look like risk. In a closed work environment that makes use of command and control management along with individual objectives and bonuses, they will each often think the other is quite insane. You can expect quite a bit of discord. This is seen as inevitable in a lot of companies.

Many managers do not understand that people have different motivations. They seem to think that people are motivated if they share the same motivation model as themselves. They assume that others are not motivated if they have a different motivation model.

Attempts to motivate people in this situation make things worse. It is like going abroad and shouting louder at non English speakers. The volume will not help if they are simply speaking a different language. You need to learn the language of the people you are dealing with.

Inspiration is a principle and motivation is a process.

Do you prefer to see the big picture or the details? In some contexts it is good to see the big picture and in others it is better to see the details. Are you steering a ship or are you figuring out how to fix the rudder?

It is really down to your preference and specific skills and abilities. You are neither right nor wrong, just fulfilling a different role in whatever you are doing. Society tends to reward one as if it were more important than the other. They are, in truth, symbiotic.

You may have a preference for the big picture or the detail. This preference could be argued to be dependant on context or on timing.

Timing: The assumption is "first big picture then details". Figure out what to do then worry about the details of how to do it.

Context: Big picture on the bridge of a ship and detail in the engine room.

There are situations that demand that people see big picture and details at the same time in order to make sense of what is happening and take necessary action.

In teams and projects we need to decide if it needs to be the same person or different people, depending on the size and complexity of the task.

The distinction that we are dealing with right now in the world in almost all walks of life is the distinction between those who want to preserve and those who want to explore. Both are strong instincts. Both are filters that determine how individuals see the world.

We sometimes have to pretend that temporary things are not temporary at all. We build a reality around us for the sake of our own progress. We make models of the world and pretend they are real.

This is a tool to let us deal with the fluidity of reality. We know all is constantly changing like the hands of a clock. We say it is twenty past two on the 11th of January 2009, even though we know that the time is constantly changing.

You ask me the time; I hear your request, consult my watch and tell you what time it was when I looked. You hear me and are satisfied. We agree to pretend that "now" exists even though it does not.

I find it helps to think of it like a climber negotiating an enormous rock face. We make these transient permanencies like pitons in reality. They are true and they hold us to the rock face while we climb but we have to move on.

There is no use cursing a piton six meters back because it is no use to you now and cursing the hand that drove it in. It was there when you needed it. It served its purpose and held true which is why you are up here.

(This is something that should be borne in mind when you plan or retrospect.)

You could go back down and get it and bring it back to drive it in here, but you would waste a lot of time. Besides you have a bottomless bag of pitons at your side. Each one you drive in allows you to move on and makes itself obsolete. Nevertheless, pitons are always a good idea. The individual one is behind you but idea of hammering in the next one to hold your weight is sound.

The only thing that is really an absolute is that there is always change.[44]

Although you may not use the same pitons again you have learned a lot about where to place them, how to drive them in and when to step off them.

We can appreciate the idea of keeping a recipe but not the meal.

My job for many years has been to introduce change. I introduce Agile methodologies to projects, teams and

---

44 And as my granny used to say – the more things change the more they stay the same.

organisations. I witness much potential and real conflict between well meaning people. Almost always it is between people who see themselves as arguing opposites but who are, in reality, just expressing two sides of the same coin.

In many cases it is people expressing views from parallel positions, believing erroneously that these are conflicting opinions. This knowledge helps one negotiate settlement in these situations.

When you are for or against things you start to make presuppositions in order to justify your stance. You start ignoring possibilities.

What many people who provide inspiration and leadership can do is to rise above it and look at it from different perspectives. They can imagine a change in context. They are confident enough in themselves to stand on their own and do not need to define themselves by anything or anyone else's success or failure. They are interested in what is possible rather than in proving themselves right.

When you are content to be simply yourself
and don't compare or compete,
everybody will respect you.
                    (Lao Tzu)

Competition

There is an element of competition introduced into our lives at an early age. At its best it produces star athletes and at its worst it produces bullies. As a parent and as a methodologist I have listened to and read Alfie Kohn's thoughts on competition with great interest.[45] In the same context I have great respect for Tim Field[46] whose work on bullying is a cornerstone and whose book "Bully In Sight" is a must read for anyone who deals with people.

Alfie Kohn quotes a number of experiments in which people, adults and children, were asked to come up with solutions, ideas and deliverables. People who were given competition as part of the brief did not do as well as those who were just asked to come up with the very best they could do.

The conclusion is that competition does not achieve what we think it does. It tends to stifle creativity, focus us on ourselves rather than the task and lead us down perilous routes.

If we try to introduce change in a way that leads people to justify what they have been doing, we have failed before we start. We must create an atmosphere where we are not condemning the old system. We are simply changing the context. We have all, by now, realised that the blame game is toxic.

What use is a compass without a needle?

When the Tao is lost, there is goodness.
When goodness is lost, there is morality.
When morality is lost, there is ritual.
Ritual is the husk of true faith,
the beginning of chaos.
(Lao Tzu)

This leads us on to the idea of hierarchies. The Tao represents a meta principle. It is at the top of the hierarchy. Goodness is a specific function of the Tao; morality is a specific function of

45 http://www.alfiekohn.org/index.html
46 http://www.successunlimited.co.uk/bio.htm

goodness. Ritual is a function of morality. Ritual for its own sake is the beginning of chaos.

In terms of our working lives, process is ritual. It is fine as long as you have not lost the path back to the principles. If you have lost a line of sight to the principles you need to re-establish it.

Process will lead you to disaster if you do not know how to change it as the context changes. If principles are guiding you it is easier to be flexible with process. Principles give you the confidence to question the process and connect back to the intent.

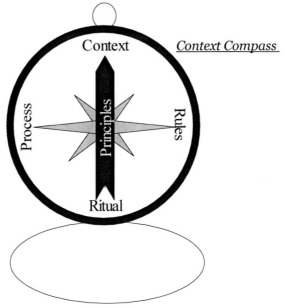

If you have only seen a compass with no needle or you do not understand the principle of a compass, you might end up thinking the N on the face always points north. You need to have a needle and understand the principles. In life, the principles are the needle that points north to the context.

Conclusion

We can cling on to the lessons of the past without clinging on to the past.

If you want to surf the current reality and inspire yourself and everyone around you, remember that:

- You put up these temporary walls in order to give yourself time and space to work – you can take them down or move them any time you want.
- You put these metaphors in place to drown out the immensity of reality so that you could concentrate – you can look beyond them when you are ready.
- You are a creature adapted to change and you understand it - you can have different results if you try new things.

When we have confidence in where we are and how we got there, we are in a position to let go of these temporary boundaries. We can explore and evaluate leaps of faith. We can formulate and test hypotheses. We know what to let go and what to hold on to. We are free to trust our intuition[47] and intellect.

If you want to become an inspirational leader and colleague, you must remember that:

- If you can keep your mind open and refrain from being for or against, you will be unfettered and you will find more opportunities in most situations and people.
- No matter how well you understand something there is always more to be learned.
- You must use your wisdom not your prejudices to inform your thinking and you must know the difference.

---

47 http://www.gladwell.com/blink/

- You must be able to accept that what you have been doing or thinking was fine in that context but as the context changes you must be able to change your response.
- You must be aware of your own filters and be able to judge new ideas on their merit rather than through the fear that they might challenge something you hold dear.
- You must be aware that the truth is context dependent and to recognise it you must be an uncarved block, neutral, objective, open to new ideas and ways of thinking.
- You must be able to challenge your beliefs and flow with the context.
- You must make a distinction between yourself and your beliefs, methods and prejudices.

Do this and you will find that you will enable yourself and other people to embrace new ways while holding on to the value, honour and internal consistency of what they have been doing. This primarily involves separating the intent and idea from the artefacts. It involves giving credit where credit is due and recognising the diversity of approach of those around you as an advantage rather than a challenge.

Balance

*"Life is like riding a bicycle.
To keep your balance you must keep moving"*
Albert Einstein

Status Quo is a rock band

When I talk about creating and maintaining balance I am not advocating that you try to maintain a status quo. I am saying that you need to know how to compensate for change.

The principle of balance is this: as change happens you understand its consequence and know what you need to do in order to keep that change from tipping things into chaos.

Risk management is not risk aversion. It is balancing the risk against the benefit. We used to call it cost benefit analysis.

Process and state

When all the rhetoric over methodologies dies down and there is only you and something to do, your ability to do it, whatever it is, depends on your balance.

Can you stand firmly in the centre and ask these questions?

- How do you balance skills against the task?
- How do you balance the need and the resource?
- How do you balance ambition and possibility?
- How do you balance aspiration and pragmatism?
- How do you balance push and pull?
- How do you balance investment for the future against capital spend?
- How do you balance assets and liabilities?
- How do you maintain your poise and equilibrium so that you can start again the next time?

Balance

I believe Richard Bandler to be a genius. He was the co-creator of NLP, Neuro Linguistic Programming. It is based on linguistics, heuristics, psychology, philosophy, practical observation and curiosity. The reason I think he is a genius is that he constantly pushes the boundaries of his reality in interesting and sometimes alarming ways and then balances his findings against the reality the rest of us perceive. In that balance he has created insights, tools and answers to some of the most vexing problems we face.

The tool I want to highlight here is the ability to differentiate between states and processes.

Many of us are tempted to think of happiness as a state. NLP points out that happiness is a nominalisation. This means that it is a process incorrectly labelled as a state. It is a noun describing a verb. Happiness is being happy. Being happy is a process therefore happiness is a process.

Many of us are tempted to think that if we can maintain the conditions that make us happy we will then have achieved permanent happiness. The world begs to differ. Even if you have achieved happiness and the external conditions remain static, something else, in your internal make-up and ongoing needs, will change.

If you have ever read anyone's account[48] of heroin addiction, you will know that the way addictive things work is as follows:

- You have a normal level of perception and comfort. It is

48 I can thoroughly recommend "Junk" by Melvin Burgess. It is aimed at a teenage market but it is still a compelling adult read. It is full of compassion and clear, concise writing. It appears to have a degree of authenticity by being a fictional account based on real people and situations. http://www.amazon.co.uk/Puffin-Teenage-Fiction-Melvin-Burgess/dp/0140380191

your baseline.
- You introduce a drug like heroin and you get a high. It masks all the little pains and worries that are part of life. You are brought to a different level of consciousness and, from what I hear, it is pretty terrific.
- The drug wears off.
- You go back to your norm. Only your norm is no longer in the place it was. You are more aware of the little worries and pains and, from your subjective perspective, you are under the weather.
- You take some more drugs to take the edge off.
- This time you need more drugs to give you the same high because you are starting from further back.
- When you come back down from this high you are even further back.
- After a while you need the drug just to achieve what used to be your norm.
- After another while you need massive amounts of the drug in order to gain just a brief respite.
- This messes with your perception of reality to an extent from which it is difficult to recover.

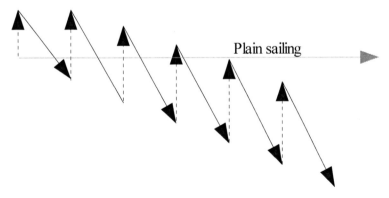

Addiction Changes Perception

Balance

If something else, like money, power, pleasure, sex or control, is substituted for heroin, then the same process is observed. We need more and more of the drug to give us a hit and to keep us in the same state. When more and more of the same is piled on it only seems to force us to lose ground. Alarming and perverse as it may seem, it is a principle of our perception of state. Too much sugar makes you sick.

The solution is to:

1. Recognise where your norm currently is.
2. Establish where you would like it to be.
3. Understand and accept that you can move it.

Since the experience is subjective, your job is to calm irrational worries and self harm and replace them with confidence and kindness to yourself. It is the path to happiness which runs through success and taking advantage of your advantages.

Once you know where the path to happiness and success lies you straddle it and achieve balance. Balance too is a process not a state. As with happiness balance can be achieved but you must work to maintain it. As with happiness if you pursue it you are always going to be pursuing it.

Have you ever balanced glasses on a tray or played one of those games where you have to get ball bearings into a hole by tilting a board around?

To be successful you need to learn:
✔ What balance feels like.
✔ What imbalance feels like.
✔ The critical point at which one tips into the other.

Balance

This tells you:
- ✔ When you need take action to maintain balance.
- ✔ What latitude of action you have whilst balanced.
- ✔ What action to take to maintain balance or rebalance.

Knowing these helps you to find equilibrium.

This equally applies to the commercial world. Your company may be chugging along quite happily but external events, technology, the economy, the market and public opinion are in a constant state of flux. Internal events mirror this. Your process which was great for the last project, customer or production team, is no longer working because all of these are variables that are moving and changing too.

Too much market share without the means to satisfy it can crush a company as surely as no sales at all. If your resources are spread too thin nothing gets delivered. If you produce more than you can sell you will end up with your assets tied up in a warehouse as inventory.

Lean manufacturing based on the observations of W Edwards Deming seeks to address this problem. Lean recognises seven wastes[49] and seeks to achieve balance in the system by learning to see and eliminate them all the time.

If you have ever played tennis or any racquet sport, you know that there is a sweet spot in the racket. You know when you have hit the ball well, even before it leaves the strings. You

---

49 The Seven Wastes
Rework – Eliminate by reducing defects to zero
Overproduction- Eliminate by making just what the customer orders
Transport – Eliminate by moving appropriate processes close to each other
Waiting – Eliminate by creating smooth flow
Inventory – Eliminate by delivering just in time
Motion – Eliminate by improving ergonomics of workplace
Over-processing – Eliminate by using right tools for the job

feel it in your arm. All around that sweet spot are areas which slice, spin, over hit and a variety of terms that tennis players are familiar with. The last thing you do is stand around admiring the lovely shot you just made, no matter how good, because the game is still on and the ball is probably on its way back.

You apply the same thing to business as to life, sport and the search for happiness. You learn how to achieve and maintain balance. You learn about what you are balancing and the effect of your actions on that balance.

Balance on a high-wire is about knowing whether you are walking a tightrope or a slack wire. If it is a tightrope you move your centre of balance over the wire by moving your body; on a slack wire you move the rope under your centre of balance by using your feet to move the position of the rope.

Using tightrope technique on a slack wire will cause the rope to swing out from under you. Using a slack wire technique on a tightrope will cause you to jump off to the right or left. Stand perfectly still on either and you will fall off. If you use a pole to help spread out your centre of mass you must hold it in the balanced centre or it will become a liability.

In business you can think of a methodology as the means to move either your centre of mass over the rope or move the rope under your centre of gravity. It is essential that you know which sort of wire you are walking. It is also essential to know that the tension in the wire can change and that you must change your tactics and strategy to stay aloft.

You can think of the process as a pole. You must know what it is there for and what it is doing for you. You must know how to change your grip on it so it does not drag you over.

Balance

Whatever problem you have, it will probably be a matter of balance. Things that go out of balance have consequences.

Feedback loops and balance

The difference between you, me and a high-wire artist is sensitivity to feedback. As with all things, the true expert perceives subtle distinctions. He feels slight shifts in his own weight, air currents and movements in the rope. He knows how to adjust and maintain balance. His feedback loops are shorter than yours or mine. We would be falling before we worked out that we had leaned too far to compensate.

The shorter the feedback loop the more responsive you can be. For the feedback loop to be short you need to be able to process and evaluate what is actually happening and take corrective action within the time frame.

Imagine the high-wire walker again. If his feedback loop waits until his centre of mass is a metre out of alignment he has to take huge corrective action. Unless he gets that exactly right he will swing out to the other side and have to take larger corrective action and in an escalation of action and reaction will quickly get out of control.

If, on the other hand, he can know when he is a fraction of a millimetre out of balance and correct immediately, his corrective action is small and much less risky. He may do more frequent corrective action but he never works as hard, all because his feedback loops are small and well under control.

There is also the small matter that he can distinguish feedback from noise; and that he understands what the feedback means.

He knows his objective is to walk along the wire to the other side and perhaps he has to juggle or stand on his head in the middle. The fact that he has sensitivity to what is really going on, not what he might wish was going on, and because his feedback loops are short he gets there with much less effort than someone who is swinging wildly and constantly pulling things back from the edge of disaster.

Balance - prioritising

When I do a consultancy I am often asked to prescribe a process. This is anathema to me. The process I recommend is:

Know how to know what to notice and then notice it.

What works here for this project has no guarantee of working on the next one. Your only hope lies in principle. The principle of priority is a good friend when you are involved in creating and maintaining balance.

I attended a time management course many years ago. One thing in particular stuck in my mind and it has been my constant ally since then. It was a little table for prioritising. You may well know it, but it is one of those principles that are pure gold dust.

Balance

Important Not Urgent	Urgent Important
Not important Not urgent	Urgent Not Important

Important — Urgent →

Important-Urgent Classic Quadrants

You distinguish between the urgent and the important. If something is **Not Important and Not Urgent** it clearly has no priority. If something is **Urgent and Not Important,** similarly it does not really have a high priority. Now, many people think that things that are **Urgent and Important** are higher priority than **Important and not Urgent**. This would seem to make sense.

Imagine what happens though, if you always deal with **Urgent and Important** stuff. In that description the urgency is taking precedence over the importance. This is what happens and what will keep happening as everything important makes its way to the urgent quadrant unless you take action to prevent it.

Is that how you really want to work? I imagine you would rather spend your time taking a balanced, skilled approach doing things properly once rather than constantly fire-fighting and cobbling things together under pressure. Things that will come back to haunt you.

Now imagine that you ignore the **Urgent and Important** stuff and concentrate on the **Important but not yet Urgent** stuff. You might get in a little hot water for a short while but most urgent stuff is urgent because it has not been done. It has not been done, generally, because it is not really that important or because someone has just knee jerked that it is.

Usually the measure of importance for things in this quadrant is really not that objective. Mostly things we see as **Urgent and Important** are really just urgent. The urgency has become confused with importance. You use judgement.

For instance if it is a tax return that will have severe penalties for not being done, you should do it. If it is a monthly report that has no real value other than someone loud requested it, then you could take the swift caning and not do it. In its place you could get on with something important. This will never become urgent and you will do a better job in the more relaxed environment of **Important Not Urgent**.

Now you will undoubtedly find yourself with a big box of **Urgent and Important** stuff that you will tell me must be done. Your job and the future of western civilisation depend on it. I understand. I have been there. We all have. There is a strain of management that thinks that this is a good state to have everyone in all the time. These remind me of people who argue that they drive better when they are drunk - they are off balance on both ends of the pole.

If you have this situation there are two things I advise.

First action: For each thing ask is it really, really important or is it just urgent. You can do this by looking at relative importance across both boxes. Some things in your **Urgent and Important** box are not really as important as anything in your ***Important Not Urgent*** box and the urgency is coming from someone throwing their weight about.

If you start talking about relative importance, many of these people are happy to think it is their idea to promote stuff from the ***Important Not Urgent*** box to the front of the queue.

Remember that you should not really worry about these people being self important. You are concerned about taking yourself and your team out of a stressful situation and into a relaxed and productive one.

Often, just by writing all the things to be done down on a list and prioritising them relative to each other, can be enough to get you working on the stuff in the ***Important Not Urgent*** box.

Second action: For each thing that is really ***Important and Urgent,*** ask is there any way it can be pushed back into the ***Important but Not Urgent*** box? Is there a workaround that will satisfy the objective?

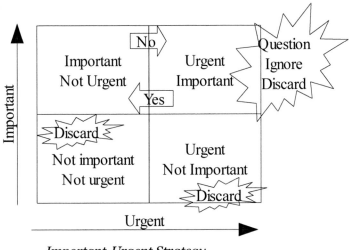

Important-Urgent Strategy

For example take that report. Perhaps your boss is only really interested in one figure for this month and the rest of the report would be fine later in the week. You might find that he is always only interested in a couple of figures on the report and the rest has always been window dressing.

I have always been amazed at how cooperative people are when you go and talk to them about their objectives and how you might cut down their work or improve the quality of data they have to sift through. I learned it early as a systems analyst converting paper systems to electronic systems.

So much is done just because that it the way it is done. "We get all the loan repayment reports so we can add them up and calculate the budget for next month. "What's that you say? You could just give us a grand total and the projections worked out for us without a four hundred page printout?". Many people are trapped in the **Urgent and Important** trap themselves and welcome a leg up over the wall.

As a systems developer I have also found that the same thing applies to requirements. Get at the objective and you will find a compromise that allows everyone to win while you postpone the bells and whistles until you have the time and they have the priority. You may even find that that they are no longer necessary.

Sometimes the workaround works better than you or your customer expects. Once out of a state of urgency everyone has the space to think rather than react.

Stress and balance

I recently heard Richard Bandler asserting that people get stupid when they are stressed. This is another principle that my own observations bear out.

Although you will find people who will tell you that they operate better under stress, it is worth investigating what they mean by stress and what they mean by better. I invite you to start observing this as empirically as you can.

As I mentioned earlier, some people assure me that they drive better when they have had a few drinks. What is really happening is that their senses are dulled and they are not as aware of what is going on. Their perception is that they are better because they are not as attuned to imbalance. This can have tragic consequences.

I have also seen individuals striding around in their element during crisis. In reality they are adding nothing but they feel important and needed. I have even found people who deliberately encourage crisis because they are convinced it gives them a chance to shine. Unfortunately this type of behaviour is often rewarded by short-sighted management and is one of the major strategies in **the other game**.

At best they are seeking credit by deliberately creating imbalance in a situation where they know they or somebody else will rebalance things. At worst they do not care whether things balance or not, they want to thrive on confusion and substitute reporting it, for actually getting anything done.

Stress on purpose

A sense of purpose or excitement is often perceived as stress, leading some people to deduce that stress is good.

If you know someone is depending on you or if you know that what you are doing is going to make a difference, it can keep you focussed. If someone is eagerly anticipating delivery, it does tend to encourage good work and attention to detail.

Conversely if you know that what you are doing is just for the sake of form and will never see the light of day, it is hard to care, no matter how urgent it is made.

There is a huge difference between stress and purpose. Stress is counter-productive and causes you to lose focus. Purpose with a clearly defined outcome promotes success.

Skills, tools, process

These things can easily be confused and it is important that they are unconfused. Let's examine them.

Although skills can make use of tools and process, they are independent of tools and process. Skills and tools are useful in any process and are more desirable.

The more useful the skill, the more independent it is of a tool or situation. A very skilful programmer is language independent, because he or she understands the principles of programming and can apply them to any language.

A skilled communicator is also independent of language. I have a French friend who speaks no English but can communicate very effectively with my non French speaking visitors. He uses rapport naturally. His meaning is clear from his tone, expression, gesture and incredible empathy with other people. I have known people to swear he was speaking English, they understood him so well, even though he spoke only French. This is a skill.

There are grades of skill. If you can drive a car but not a motorbike, tractor, digger, ambulance or an articulated truck, you have a driving skill, but it is not very flexible. If you can drive anything with wheels, your driving skill is more adaptable and, ultimately, more valuable. You can deal with any driving situation. Moreover you are probably safer in a car because you have seen the road from a number of perspectives. This gives you an appreciation of a more fully defined reality.

I have a cousin who can drive all of the above. Being in a car with him is probably safer than being at home by the fire with a book.

This brings me to the idea of near and far learning.

If you can only do something in a specific circumstance with a specific tool, you have near learning. Your skill stays near to this application. It is similar to only being able to drive an automatic transmission car.

If you can apply your skill in a number of circumstances with a number of tools, you have far learning. Your skill has far reaching scope - like my cousin, who can drive any vehicle, or a musician who understands music so well they can play any instrument.

This is an area where balance is often lost. Individuals and companies often put a lot of time and energy into near learning. This leads them to have an over dependence on a process or set of tools. This is imbalance. It makes it very difficult to make changes of any sort.

"The cost of training!" they chorus when change is necessary or when a new, more effective tool or process is proposed. If balance between near and far learning is maintained, this never becomes a problem, because they can adapt easily and cheaply to any tool or process.

Processes are usually associated with near learning. Tools can either be near or far. It depends on the complexity of the tool and the design of it. If a tool is complex but well designed and belongs to a set of similarly designed tools, far learning is simulated. If something changes in the set then the learning regresses to near.

Many companies seek to compartmentalise their technical people. These compartments are not just by technology but by specific application. The result is people who are never in a position to see the bigger picture. They are off balance and if the technology moves on, they find they have a set of narrow skills and will need to be completely retrained.

Programmers who understand the underlying principles of programming can adapt to any language quickly. This makes them very valuable to an organisation, because they are more likely to choose the best technology for the job.

Therefore learning based on principles has longer legs and goes further. The more general the principles the more they can be adapted and the farther they will take you safely into the future.

Base your training in principles rather than specific tools or processes.

Legs and stamina

You need to consider the consequences, in your own career, of putting all your eggs in your current company's basket. What will be the effect of specialising in their tools, processes and systems?

You need to balance your job security against your marketability. The smart money tends to be on skills with legs and stamina for the individual.

Balance

A smart company will realise that it has a wider pool of talent to draw on inside the company if its people are mobile. It will also be able to draw on a wider pool outside the company if its technology, tools and process are not restricted to a small group of virtuosos and prima-donnas. It will be able to attract those smart people who have invested in versatile, far-learning skills.

Companies who look for Java Programmers with five years experience or people qualified in the latest planning tool are really missing the point. Their job advertisements will only attract near learning skills.

Doing something repeatedly for year after year in the same environment just gives you the same years experience over and over again. I look for people who have worked in a number of environments and who have tried a lot of approaches. They literally have more experience.

Skills with legs and stamina are those which are useful generally to companies, regardless of specialisation. They are not going to go out of fashion. You are not tightly coupled to the technology, methodologies, processes or tools that are currently in vogue. You can use the latest things, of course, but you resist painting yourself into a corner.

Useful skills tend to be more principle based rather than application based. If you can balance the needs of your employer with your own needs, you have it made and everyone is a winner.

Some employers are fearful of developing their people along these lines. They are afraid that if their people are well trained with generic skills, they will leave for a better offer. This immediately signifies an imbalance to me.

Why are they so sure their people will jump ship when they get another offer? What are they doing to their people that makes them believe they will take the first opportunity to leave?

If you provide a good balanced environment you do not even have to bribe your employees with large bonuses. Almost everyone I know prefers to work in an environment where they feel they get a chance to develop. Many people, who have a decent wage, put self development and respect ahead of bags of cash.

It is mainly when something is out of balance that people head for the door. For instance in the IT world, many of the best people change job precisely in order to keep their skills current.

History has shown that true loyalty can not be extorted or bought. The more secure that people feel, the more they feel that they are spending their time doing something worthwhile and the more they feel that their life is balanced the more likely they are to feel and exhibit real loyalty.

Fulcrums

There are few things that we have discovered that are as useful as the fulcrum.

fulcrum
A - The support about which a lever turns.
B - One that supplies capability for action.

Balance

In a first class lever the fulcrum is between the load and the effort.

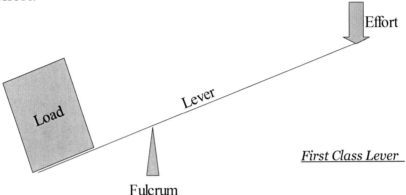

First Class Lever

Fulcrum

When you want to move something, the closer to the load the fulcrum is, the easier it is to move the lever and lift the weight.

There is a point at which you have moved the fulcrum near enough to the load to make it possible for you to move the load. Any more effort moving the fulcrum closer to the load can be considered waste. After this it is moving from the point of possibility towards ease.

It is a matter of cost benefit. Will the gain in ease justify the effort of moving the fulcrum further?. You may have enough leverage to get on with it.

When the load is between the effort and the fulcrum we have a second class lever.

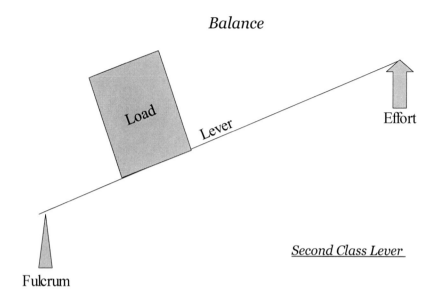

Balance

Load

Lever

Effort

Fulcrum

<u>*Second Class Lever*</u>

A third class lever puts the effort between the load and the fulcrum:

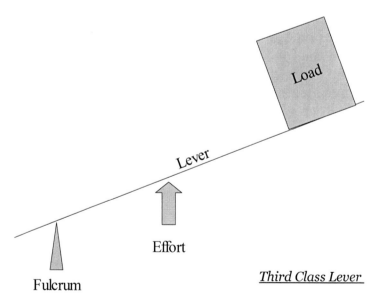

Load

Lever

Effort

Fulcrum

<u>*Third Class Lever*</u>

Principle of the fulcrum: The effort multiplied by its distance from the fulcrum equals the load multiplied by its distance from the fulcrum.

112

I.e. To move one kilogram of load you need to exert one kilogram of pressure if both the effort and the load are equidistant from the fulcrum.

The lever is in equilibrium when the load and effort balance each other.

The following table demonstrates the relationship for an arbitrary lever 5 meters long and the load of 500kg.

Class of lever	Distance of fulcrum from load (meters)	Distance of effort from fulcrum (meters)	Distance of effort from load (meters)	Effort required to lift load
First	0.1	4.9	5	10.2+kg
	2.5	2.5	5	500+kg
Second	0.1	5	4.9	10+kg
	2.5	5	2.5	100+kg
Third	5	0.1		25000+kg
	5	5		500+kg

There are a number of ways to look at this.
- If the effort is constant then the position of the fulcrum can affect the amount of load it can move.
- If the load is constant the position of the fulcrum can affect the effort required to move it.
- If the load and effort are constant there is an optimal position for the fulcrum
- If you do not know how to move the fulcrum you have to change the load, the effort or the length of the lever.
- Under certain circumstances second class levers are more

efficient than first class levers
* Although they obey the same principles all the levers behave differently

A lot of my metaphors are DIY based[50] because I have spent the last number of years renovating a French farmhouse.

Therefore, here are some examples of types of lever I use on a daily basis

* First class
  o Triceps
  o Hammer claw
  o Pliers
  o Crowbar

* Second class
  o Wheelbarrow
  o Wrench
  o Crowbar

* Third class
  o Broom
  o Hammer
  o Shovel
  o Crowbar[51]

Through all my DIY I discovered that when it came to moving something heavy I had to watch my back. This made knowing about fulcrums and levers a necessity and did they ever turn out to be my best friends.

---

50 DIY is a UK term which stands for "Do IT Yourself". It refers to people who create or repair things for themselves without the aid of paid professionals. My DIY was mainly about home improvement and house renovation.

51 Go on, have a guess at which tool I use on almost every job!

Balance

You would be amazed at what I lifted, moved, hoisted and positioned. Having listened to everyone telling me that it was impossible without a large machine, I lifted a broken beam and several tons of roof 5 meters above my head, with one hand and two pieces of wood. Oh and a fulcrum.

It was an amazing thing to consider that a little know-how had allowed me to fashion a simple tool to do a horribly difficult thing. I had wrestled with the problem of how to lift the beam for over a year.

Watching the huge beam, that had been broken and sagging for decades, begin to lift, I thought of Archimedes. The answer was misleadingly simple to behold.

The lever is a simple but powerful principle. I had merely scaled up that principle and it had held.

I want to apply this insight to project management and to life in general.

For the sake of the metaphor we will say that the lever is time, the load is the work that needs to be done and the effort is the resource available.

It is consistent with the iron triangle of project management. Time, Cost, Requirements. If you have a big weight and little effort you must change the length of the lever. If you have only one lever you must either change the load or the effort. Methodologies are all ways of applying the principles of project management, just as classes of levers are ways of applying the laws of levers.

If I stretch the metaphor a bit, I can see that command and control usually demands more effort and is all about force. It probably works as a third class lever.

- The fulcrum is fixed at the end of the lever
- The load is never lightened. Requirements are captured up front, costed and signed off.
- Lengthening the lever (time) just makes things worse. New features creep in, the initial requirements change and the plan becomes more and more difficult to maintain.
  1. The effort (resource) required must always be equal to or more than the full load.
- There are times when the requirements, resource and time are an exact fit and this approach will at least work.
- When all you have is an expensive hammer everything becomes a nail[52].

If it were a second class lever:

- The fulcrum is fixed at the end of the lever
- The load can be moved using less effort by
  → Moving the load closer to the front of the lever – I.e. doing more up front design and getting it right
  → Increasing the length of the lever – I.e. more time
- It requires you to be able to move the load around.
- If you move the load too close to the effort you start losing efficiency

These other two have the similarity that they do not change the position of the fulcrum or the lever with respect to each other.

The first class lever has flexibility and reminds me of Agile:

---

52 Abraham Maslow (1908-70): His most famous theory is the hierarchy of human needs, but he also used this hammer metaphor to describe the effect the other famous metaphor, the silver bullet, and the importance of using the right tool for the job not just what is available.

- The fulcrum changes in order to make best use of the effort and the lever available – makes best use of the resources and time available.

All three classes of lever work. The constraint is that they can not cheat the primary principle:

$$(\text{Load}) \times (\text{distance to fulcrum})$$
$$\text{must equal}$$
$$(\text{effort}) \times (\text{distance to fulcrum})$$

There is a dilemma associated with the iron triangle. There is an inter-relationship between time, requirements and effort which means that you can not move one of the corners without moving one or both of the others. If you insist on all three staying static in a changing world, the inevitable outcome is a reduction in quality.

If you do not have enough resource you must either spend more time on it or you must de-scope what you are doing. This is somewhat of a problem for traditional projects as they have negotiated a budget up front and they will be penalised if they take longer than planned.

If we can use the idea of a first class lever we have a way of breaking this deadlock. First of all we have to identify our fulcrum. You might be tempted to say that it is *Quality*. I thought that at first but quality is the outcome of the system.

You can decide you want less or more quality. Quality is a measurable outcome not an enabler[53]. Although I have myself, in the past, used the argument that quality is the fourth dial, I

---

53 Although good quality code is easier and cheaper to maintain and quality should be built into the process, quality is still a negotiable requirement that has a cost and takes time to implement.

admit that this is a sleight of hand. Quality is really a non functional requirement. It belongs with security, maintainability and the other non functional aspects of what you are doing.

No, we are looking for something else.

Balance and release

I have often noticed that imbalance is a result of things being stored up. There is pain when these things seek a release in an attempt to find balance again. All things flow toward balance. If this seems a little new age or spiritual, think again. It is the basis for physics.

Have you ever had to unravel a ball of wool, a garden hose, a kite string? The tighter it is all held the more impossible it is to see the pattern in the tangle and the individual strings. When you shake it a bit and loosen the threads you start to see a way forward. You continue to loosen and then comes the almost magical point where you can see how the threads are related to each other and the tangle becomes manageable.

I notice that when I have let stress build up, my body escalates its objections and attempts to find release in order to force balance. It can be tiredness, a headache, ill humour, irritability or a sickness of some sort. I find that going for a run or a walk tends to work. Things that had become toweringly difficult and complex unravel and separate. By counterbalancing the stress with a complimentary sort of work my mind loosens the threads.

Organisations have the same tendencies. When you observe problems there is little point in putting on a band aid, you need to find out what is out of balance. You need to find out what is the thing you need to rebalance. It is an ongoing process. You need to lighten one side, add weight to the other or move the fulcrum.

If bad stuff has been stored up for a long time the balancing will take longer and more drastic action. If it is just the ebb and flow of entropy it is easier to deal with.

What is being stored up?
· Resentment?
· Worry?
· Repressed creative instinct?
· Boredom?
· Frustration?
· Thwarted ambition?
· Necessary change?
· People's own lives?
· Free speech?
· Technical ability?
· Communication?
· Maintenance?
· Fun?

When you know what is causing the imbalance, you can start looking for the counterbalance and the constraints, values and priorities that will tell you what to adjust.

Counterbalances

When you have found out what is out of balance you may find you have many things to balance. You must do some analysis

You need to untangle the dependencies. What I mean is that there is a temptation to link things that do not have reciprocal dependencies. There is a tendency to ascribe effect to the wrong cause. This is lazy and will store up more trouble than you will be able to deal with. It will appear to present seemingly intractable problems, which any intervention will only exacerbate.

You may find that you have a list of things that appear to be out of balance scattered around your organisation or team. It may look something like (Step 1 below) when you have identified the things that are of concern.

Step 1 - Identify the things that need to be balanced

These concerns could represent:

- Importance
- Priority
- Complexity
- Stability
- Productivity
- Skill
- Urgency
- Effort
- Difficulty
- Responsiveness
- Tiredness
- Process

Balance

Your organisation will have different stresses in different places. Resources and management attention will be focused in different ways on these things. Changing them without having some basic understanding of the effect will feel like playing that children's game where you bash one thing down and four more pop up[54].

It will continue to look like this if you are balancing the wrong things against each other. Things will get stored up and harder to balance when crisis strikes.

You will need your powers of observation and analysis.
- What are the things that affect each others balance?
- Search for reciprocal relationships. When you strengthen A does B weaken? Now does A weaken when you strengthen B or does A have that sort of reciprocal relationship with C?

When you find these things that are each others counterbalance you have a practical means of adjusting them. Furthermore you have a set of guidelines for how much to adjust them.

I have found that there are principles to the art of balance:

✔ Everything has a counterbalance
✔ Everything you adjust has impact on its counterbalance.
✔ If A is counterbalanced to B then you can affect the balance by adjusting either A or B. Which is counterbalance depends on where you are standing.
✔ You can affect the balance by moving the fulcrum. In many cases this is the relative focus and priority you give to either end.

This respects the third law of motion. For every action there is

---
54 Whack-a-mole I think.

an equal and opposite reaction. The advantage you have is that once you know this relationship you can adjust either end.

This is a pattern repeated throughout the natural world.

When I was at school I was amazed by this reciprocity. Just take electromagnetism for instance.

Pushing an electrical current through a wire creates a magnetic field. The way we were told to remember was to take the right fist and stick out the thumb. If the thumb indicates the direction of the current, the fingers indicates the direction of the magnetic field.

This was an exciting discovery. Who was it that made the leap to check out the counterbalance?[55] A magnet rotated around a wire, or more commonly inside a wire coil, generates an electric current. Welcome to power on demand.

Electricity and magnetism are counterbalances to each other. They are not opposites, you will notice, but if you adjust one, the other will change. They have a reciprocal arrangement.

There are other things that are counterbalances but not opposites.

F Matthias Alexander (1869-1955) was an Australian actor. In the 1890's he began to lose his voice. A succession of doctors, specialists and voice coaches failed to provide an effective treatment. His voice was his profession so he decided to take matters into his own hands.

---

55 Michael Faraday(1791-1867) discovered the principle of magnetic induction in 1831. It was the wonderfully named Hippolyte Pixii (1808-1835) who had the idea of spinning a magnet and built the first A/C generator in 1832.

Perhaps because he was not a doctor or a specialist he approached the whole thing differently. He bought a lot of mirrors and observed himself. He discovered that when he performed he changed his posture. He discovered that it was in fact his unconscious posture that was constricting his breathing and affecting his voice. By consciously changing his posture he corrected the breathing and thus the voice problem.

Now the twist comes. Our posture changes our breathing but our breathing changes our posture. You can try this yourself.

The next time you go for a walk try breathing first from the top of your chest and then after a while from the bottom of your stomach. Notice the posture changes.

✔ Health can affect mental state. Mental state can affect health. You may be able to help an aching back and bad digestion by being cheerful!

These relationships are fascinating. They translate into all aspects of life. When I help companies change process models there are always results that surprise people. I use the principles of balance.

Instead of observing cause and effect many people are repeating a mantra of some kind to themselves. When you help them to think about it, initially they may hate you for upsetting a perfectly comfortable theory with the facts. In time, almost all come to realise that it is easier to practice observation and effective action based on those observations.

The way I recommend is to notice what gets rigorous in order for something else to be flexible and what must be flexible in order for something else to be rigorous.

In this sense I welcome problems.

In my experience problems are caused by people trying to move the balance and the counterbalance in the same direction. It looks to me like trying to get both ends of a see-saw to go up at the same time.

For instance companies wanting lots of huge detailed plans and responsiveness at the same time causes problems. If you want these sorts of plans you will find it hard to change direction. If you rely on responsiveness you need to have clearly defined long term objectives but encourage less detailed plans as to how to achieve them. This allows you to respond to change.

One side goes up while the other comes down.

In software development when the testing is left until the end, adding new features and fixing problems takes much longer. To have code that is easily maintainable the testing must be comprehensive, honest and continuous.

There are many more examples of this that will be explored in volume 2.

Find the centre

The sorts of things you might find on opposite ends of these balance/counterbalance lines might be:

- Stability ---------------Responsiveness
- Productivity-----------Tiredness
- Skill---------------------Process
- Priority-----------------Effort
- Importance -----------Urgency
- Complexity------------Difficulty

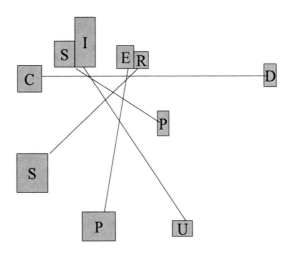

Step 2 - Pair things into balance and counterbalance

Of course each situation has its own particular dependencies and balances. These are just random examples.

- Stability-Responsiveness
  - → Is your emphasis on stability interfering with your ability to compete in the market because you can not make updates?
  - → Is your emphasis on unnecessary functionality causing too many unstable deliveries?
- Productivity-Tiredness
  - → Is your staff so tired from working extra hours that they are making more and more silly errors?
  - → Have you fractionated people's responsibilities so much that they are not spending enough quality time on things and are therefore not engaged?
- Process-Skill
  - → Is your process so proscriptive that your people are not thinking any more?
  - → Do your people have to deal with repetitive tasks that could be more easily dealt with by an automated process?
- Priority-Effort
  - → Is your management style so strong that people are unwilling to make decisions?
  - → Are there too many people making decisions that should be centralised?
- Urgency-Importance
  - → Is everything so urgent that you can see no relative importance?
  - → Is your emphasis too much on long term goals to the point that you are losing the tactical advantage?
- Complexity-Difficulty
  - → Are your requirements so complex that there is no room for creative solutions?
  - → Are your solutions focused enough on the specifics of the users?

It may look and feel like this (Step 3) and you may be tempted to balance the one thing you feel comfortable with and declare the job done. You must balance all of the pairs by bringing them into focus one at a time.

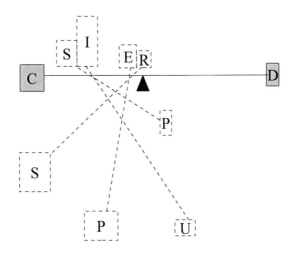

Step 3 - Find the balance point.

Balance the counterbalancing pairs, one at a time.

When you start focussing on everything you may have a situation that feels something like this (Step 4). You feel that there is a common fulcrum: You, the sole voice of sanity in a mad world.

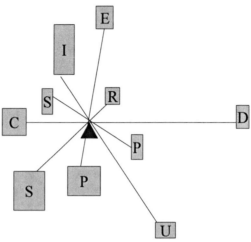

Step 4 - Become the fulcrum of all balances.

Notice when things are in balance and when change requires you to move the fulcrum.

As the fulcrum you may find yourself at the balance point of all these things. You may feel that it is all very precarious and that by changing one balance you affect them all. This is not the case.

It will help to un-wire the dependencies mentally and achieve Step 5 below. It always helps to clarify your thinking to avoid confusion.

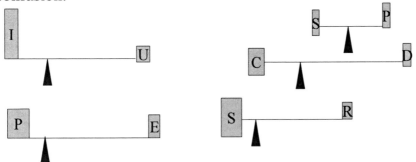

Step 5 - Un-wire the dependencies to avoid confusion.

Only balance what needs to be balanced at any one time.

Once you start seeing these things as controls that you can adjust in different ways, you will keep your thinking clear and focussed. You will also find that when you can explain clearly and rationally what you are doing then you are not alone after all. If you do the unwiring and can help people to see the trees for the woods, they tend to adjust to this model.

In summary here are the steps I am describing:

✔ Make sure you are balancing things that are actually counterbalances to each other.
✔ Check that you are balancing ***all*** of these things.
✔ Make sure you understand dependencies so that you can keep discrete things discrete.
✔ You will need to rebalance depending on culture, power shifts, priorities, structural changes, external conditions and all sorts of change.

__Balancing the Organisation__

Step 1: Identify things to be balanced

Step 2:
Balance and
Counterbalance
Pairs

Step 3:
Find the balance
Of each pair

Step 4:
Control the
fulcrum

Step 5:
Un-Wire
dependencies

130

Time for a metaphor:

I was singing on stage once. Under the lights my guitar went badly out of tune. With a sea of faces turned toward me I started to tune it.

A six string guitar has six key pegs on the end of the neck to tighten or loosen the strings thereby changing the note.

A guitar can be in relative tune. This means that the strings are in relative tune to each other but not necessarily in perfect pitch.

So I was tuning my guitar with sweaty fingers in front of all these people. I was trying to tune the G string by turning the relevant key.

Ting tung, ting tung. I twisted the key to a position I thought would correct its tuning. Nothing was happening. The note stayed flat. I gave it another twist. Ting, tung. I panicked and gave it a really good turn. Thwang. The E string broke.

All the while I had been talking to my audience. Now there was a little line of blood on my finger where the breaking string had snapped out and cut it. I yelped. They laughed. They thought it was part of the act.

I started to explain to the audience what was happening and reassured them that this sort of thing frequently happened to

Segovia[56] himself.

While I tuned I began to tell them a story of how Segovia had found himself in front of the Emperor of China with a badly out of tune guitar.

Much like this, I said, as I demonstrated the lamentable state of my own out of tune instrument.

He had to decide which string was a true note, I said. Like me, he had perfect pitch. I plucked each string in turn for my audience. The top E is the closest. It is only a small fraction out. It can be fixed like this. I sang an E and tuned the guitar to it.

I continued the story telling how Segovia's guitar somehow had the strings on the wrong pegs.

Just now you saw that mine had the E string somehow connected to the key normally reserved for the G string, I said. All of Segovia's strings were connected to the wrong keys. He needed to twist all the keys and look at the effect to see which string was affected by which key.

As he did this the emperor was getting impatient, He insisted that Segovia save time by tuning all the strings at the same time and sent some retainers forward to twist wildly at the keys under the direction of the Maestro.

---

56 Andrés Segovia (1893-1987). guitarist who was hugely influential in changing the perception of the guitar from a noisy folk instrument to a classical instrument of great virtuosity.

Even Segovia had difficulty tuning them all at the same time. So he begged the emperor's indulgence and promised to make the tuning more interesting.

He told the emperor the strings: EADGBE. He told him to pick one. The emperor picked D. Segovia tuned the string with no reference to the other strings. Next came top E, followed by G, bottom E, A and finally B.

Segovia strummed the guitar to show that all the strings were in perfect pitch and in relative tune. So did I.

I thanked my audience and told them that the story had been a necessary lie to buy me time to replace the broken string and to tune my guitar. As far as I knew Segovia never met the Emperor of China.

Now if you are in business and you can imagine that there are things that have a relationship with each other like the key peg and the string. Tighten the peg and the string gives a higher note. Loosen the peg and the string gives a lower note. Pull the string and the tension of the peg increases. Let go of the string and the tension on the peg decreases.

Your strings and pegs are all mixed up.

- Importance
- Priority
- Complexity
- Stability
- Productivity
- Skill

- Urgency
- Effort
- Difficulty
- Responsiveness
- Tiredness
- Process

Someone may have made an effort to string them for you. The worst case would be that they are all strung onto one or two pegs:

- Importance-----------Urgency
- Priority----------------Urgency
- Complexity-----------Urgency
- Stability---------------Process
- Productivity----------Process
- Skill-------------------Process
- Effort----------------Urgency
- Difficulty-------------Process
- Responsiveness-----Urgency
- Tiredness------------Urgency

This is unplayable. You might be lucky and someone has had a go at making it look right:

- Stability ------------------Risk
- Productivity--------------Effort
- Skill----------------------Process
- Priority -------------------Complexity
- Importance --------------Speed
- Responsiveness----------Urgency

If this has not been as a result of the laws of balance you might be able to play but no one will recognise the tune.

You may find that when you stop doing risky things you do

not get more stability but your profitability drops.

You may find that when you demand more effort, productivity does not increase; instead everyone loses focus on what is the priority.

You seek to lessen your dependency on skill by introducing more process. You then find you have to outsource your work because the skills are gone.

Many planners give complex things priority. They may find that they have delivered a lot of complex things nobody wants.

They may find that they have missed highly profitable opportunities that they could have delivered with a fraction of the effort. Complexity or lack of it is not indicator of importance.

Important things may be carried out with haste. As the saying goes: "More haste less speed". The same could be said of haste, quality and worth.

You may see responsiveness tackled by making things urgent. Watch as the brain freeze or the panic sets in. In bad cases this can even lead to despair not responsiveness.

The result of this is that you are no longer responsive. So you crank up the urgency again. That only hides the relative importance. You prioritise the complex things to get them out of the way. This kills both speed and responsiveness.

When you check for real counterbalances you look at the things that obey the third law of motion, the reciprocal one. For every action there is an equal and opposite reaction.

You might find that acceptance of change increases responsiveness and that increased responsiveness lowers the impact of change. One goes up the other goes down.

You might find that people who work shorter hours are more productive because of the quality of their work and that just a constant pressure for productivity tires and de-motivates people . One goes up the other goes down.

You might find that by giving more priorities, effort is spread too thin. When people put more effort in they tend to focus on the highest priorities. One goes up the other comes down and vice versa.

You may find that making things more urgent diminishes their importance. It is almost as if making things more important makes people take their time to do them properly. If something can be rushed it can't be all that important. This is balance and counterbalance in action.

You might hear that the more complex the tasks you give people the more interested and engaged they become and the less difficult they find their work. You may find that by removing the complexity from difficult tasks, people are more liable to get them done.

Your balances and counterbalances may change to look like this:

- Stability------------------------Responsiveness
- Productivity--------------------Tiredness
- Skill----------------------------Process
- Priority-------------------------Effort
- Importance -------------------Urgency
- Complexity -------------------Difficulty

Now you are in a position to start adjusting:
- You know what the relationships are.
- You know where the imbalance is likely to present itself.
- You know where to look for effects of adjustment.
- You know how to measure the adjustments you make.
- You know what you want balance to look like.

Focus

When you look at something your natural inclination is to focus on it. You literally focus the light rays on photo receptive cells at the focal point of your retina, the fovea. This gives you a small sharp image.

As far back as the ancient Greeks, field of vision has fascinated scientists, philosophers, artists and anyone interested in perception. Leonardo Da Vinci was probably the first person in Europe to notice that you see only a very small area when you are focussed; and this is in direct line of sight.

Others noticed that the eye is not all that great an optical instrument and concluded that our brain must infer a lot from the input to create the image we perceive. In other words while you are focussed on something your brain uses its imagination, memory and creative faculty to fill in everything else.

When you stop focussing you become more aware of your peripheral vision. In effect your field of vision widens and you are very much more aware of movement and changes, although the focus is not sharp. Many sports people use this knowledge to improve their game and can switch between focussed (or foveal vision) and peripheral vision.

Balance

The problem with focussing on something is that you lose sight of everything else. In some circumstances this is a very good thing but for others it is disastrous. You need to be able to move your focus from one thing to the next. You need to be able to see subtle shifts and changes going on around you. These indicate those elements of balance and feedback we have been discussing.

When I manage or coach teams, I find it effective to spend time with them, fading into their background and just letting them get on with things. This way I can see and hear the subtle shifts and changes. A rookie mistake is to jump in and start telling people what to do. In effect this is like seeing a very small sharp focussed picture and inferring the rest. When you are a consultant there is a lot of pressure to do this.

I have seen some managers and consultants initially impressing their clients with much focus on detail. While they are focussed on the quick wins and the "low hanging fruit" they are always in search of, they miss obvious patterns in the weft and weave of what is going on around them. Quite often the result is confusion. Things can drift aimlessly after a while. None of the low hanging fruit turns out to be sweet. Nothing is really changed. Confidence and trust are compromised - sold out for a quick profit.

Finding and setting up self perpetuating balance is a long game. It requires patience and the ability to control focus.

Many critical things cannot be forced. They only happen when they happen. You have to be there to notice them. You shift your attention so that it is not so focussed on details and you notice the crucial patterns of behaviour. This way you can separate assumptions and habit from events that need attention.

A small piece of wood and a few drops of water applied to the correct place can crack a rock open more quickly and efficiently than a chain gang with sledgehammers.

How you decide which things to focus on and for how long is a strategy worth developing if you want to be a world class manager and a balanced worker.

Priority

Everything has a priority. When something has top priority it has everybody's focus. The result is that other things go out of focus.

As time progresses priorities change. While everybody is focussed on the top priority, other things are gaining in importance. There is a point at which aspects of the top priority are not as important as other things in the queue.

Priority is fractal. Within an item there are aspects with different priority. Unless you have packaged everything to perfection, aspects of the top priority are not as important as aspects of the next priority in line.

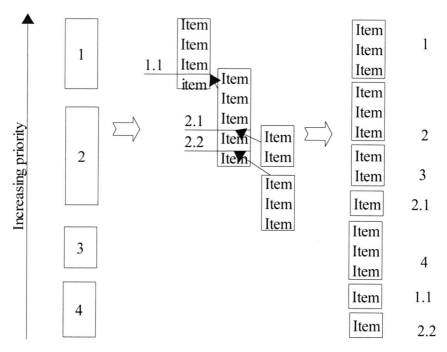

Fractal Priorities

I balance priority with simplicity. When something is a high priority, it is the very thing to simplify. Split the task down into internal priorities to clarify it.

I ask the same questions of each item in a prioritised list. What are the aspects of this thing that make it a priority? Can they be split into sub items? Do all the sub items have the same priority as the main item?

In essence, simplify it. Follow these sub-priorities until the feature that made this a priority has been delivered. This is also known as a "minimum marketable feature set" in software development.

As counter intuitive as it may seem, when something is a high priority, it is the first one that must shed bells and whistles. It must have its essential functionality delivered and not be confused by other requirements that have attached themselves to it.

I wonder if you can get an image of a tall mast ship.
- ✔ It must float.
- ✔ It must carry passengers.
- ✔ It must go from one side of this stream to the other.

"WHAT? HOLD ON A MINUTE HERE!"

"How many passengers are we talking about?"

"That stream can't be more than a couple of meters wide can it?"

"One passenger? How about a row-boat or a raft then?"

"A million passengers you say? How about a bridge? A plank across the river to get things moving?"

The illusion of a tall mast ship turned out to be made up of barnacles – opportunistic requirements.

Based on observation and experience, high priority must be decoupled from complexity. The balance you need is achieved by introducing simplicity.

Do the simplest thing possible to meet the requirements. If it is mission critical, you do not want it held up while you hand stitch the bunting. The priority is to get it in service with those critical features exposed for robust use.

Team mechanics and coaching

Do you spend your time coaching or managing?
Do you understand the difference?

How much time do you spend coaching?

- Too much and familiarity breeds contempt.
- Too little and they lose interest or think you don't care.

How much attention do you give to individuals?

- Too much and there is jealousy in the rest of the team.
- Too little and you lose trust and thrust.

Have you got a rubric to help you recognise what sort of people you are dealing with? What are their mental models and perceptions of the situation? The goal is to move the individuals in the team toward each other by encouraging tolerance of each others needs, styles and communication patterns.

I have found that by analysing this I can achieve a balance between group and individual coaching. The desirable outcome is generative behaviour. That is when the team members start coaching each other. When this happens all sorts of productive behaviour surfaces.

Way back when I did my first coaching course, I was relieved to learn that coaching theory supports playing to strengths.

Coaching is about finding what a person is good at and encouraging that strength. The theory is that it is easier to ride a horse in the direction it is already going.

If they are not good at something or not doing it, there is probably a reason - most likely they do not want to do it because it does not feel right. Why?

Is it a matter of ability and skills or is it a misconception caused by something being out of balance? If so, what is out of balance?

You are a good coach, if you can help people find direction and focus.

Generative Learning and Return on Investment

If you would like to follow a coaching approach to management, I suggest you consider some of the following:

- How will you get yourself to where you can constantly improve you own Coaching skills?
- What are the threads of coaching?
- How do you balance requirements of individuals with requirements of business?
- How much is enough? When do you give and when do you stand back and let them discover for themselves?
- What is the difference between push and pull?
- How do you know when and how to move people off a team?

Forming, storming, norming and performing:
A question I get asked by worried managers is the last one in the above list. They want to know when and how to move people off a team.

That somebody is worried about this is a good sign. The first question to ask is - what is the objective of moving people off the team?

In many big companies it is has been a hard struggle to get the company to see the value of building a capable team. Many companies want to have "plug and play" people. They prefer to ignore everything that has been learned about group dynamics.

Sometimes I have been tempted to conclude that people are moved around simply to give the machine something to do. To keep everyone sharp, so to speak. There is a belief that moving people around will help them to broaden their experience.

This rationale usually comes from organisations that are trying to impose a standard best procedure for everything, in an attempt clone standard teams. They rarely see the amusing paradox their rhetoric creates.

In some cases I have observed great teams being broken up in order to "seed" other teams with good habits. This goes back to a belief in magic and an unwillingness to understand why the good team is good in the first place. It almost never works.

The "seed" having been given this mission, generally has no idea how to do it. This person is rarely given authority, and in any case the new team has an immediate case to prove against the poor "seed".

It is only when the seed coincidentally happens to be a talented coach and knows how to bring out the strengths of the new team rather than trying to turn it in to the old team that seeding works. Even then it is not seeding – it is coaching.

There are valid reasons for moving people out of a team:

- ✔ The individual being moved wants to move.
- ✔ The individual has a rare skill-set that is needed elsewhere.
- ✔ The team itself has decided that it has run its course in its current form.
- ✔ The company works in a situation where different team sizes are dynamically required.
- ✔ The move is temporary and reciprocal to help two teams to join work together
    - ☑ In ancient Ireland the chiefs exchanged sons for training and education. This benign hostage exchange was a way to ensure cooperation between the tribes.

In the normal course of events a team is made not born.

Bruce Tuckman's model of forming, storming, norming and performing, proposed in 1965, is as good a model as I have come across to explain why good teams happen, how they happen, what they are and what to do to generate and protect them.

The really great teams I have worked with and observed did not come into being because some genius manager put these people together. They came about because some genius manager stood back and let the team "become" and provided direction when necessary.

The people who had been thrown together were given the time and space to:

✔ Form – get to know one another and explore outcomes.
✔ Storm – test each others metal.
✔ Norm - decide on roles, team structure and how to play to each others strengths
✔ Perform – do what they do well and revel in it

I have found that different teams work through these phases on different time-scales. The fastest gelling team I ever encountered took about three weeks to get to performing. It was a team of exceptionally experienced and mature individuals, many of whom already knew and trusted each other.

It is more usual for this process to take months and teams can continue gelling and improving for years.

Many teams never get beyond storming because they are not allowed to. Every time they start norming the goalposts are changed on them. Most often imbalance is constantly introduced and certain elements of the team are falsely empowered.

For instance the process police run to management or the

professionally discontented are supported in vetoing every idea.

Sometimes teams get stuck in norming. They become too focused internally and need leadership.

You do not need much in the way of metrics for a team that is storming. They generate energy from within and accept good leadership willingly.

Teams that have reached this stage will cycle around these steps more and more quickly in order to deal with change.

There appear to be roles that need to be played in every group. People are very flexible. In my observations I have noted people sliding into different roles as the need arises. I watched one guy play the team cynic when it was necessary and then the staunch defender of new ideas. Neither he nor his colleagues seemed to have any inkling that this was going on.

I have also noted that teams that include female members tend to move off the storming phase more quickly. I can only guess that this is because women do not compete for power in the same way as men and want to get on to getting the job done as soon as possible.

You will notice that even teams made up from highly skilled and mature people still need to go through these phases. The only difference I have perceived is that people who have been through it successfully seem to be more relaxed about it. They are patient and know that despite the pain of some of the earlier stages it will all come out in the wash.

So, when and how to move people off a team?

✔ Make sure you really should be moving them.
  ☑ If you want to create another similar team avoid "seeding". Get them a coach or let them visit the working team. Remember that each set of people will form a unique team.
✔ When you move people, move them at the end of a performing phase.
  ☑ Let them come back for celebrations or accolades.
  ☑ If the team has not had a performing phase and you disrupt the cycle you may compromise this team's ability to ever perform. They may not see the point in ever forming a cohesive team.
  ☑ If the team has performed for the first time and their reward is to be yanked apart, the individuals will similarly never trust you again.

You need to know where the team is in its cycle. You need to know what effect moving people will have. You need to time it correctly with the help of the team. This needs to be a change done with the team not done to it.

Consider founding flexible and effective teams, then bringing the work to them. It is more effective than trying to have plug and play teams who are expected to assemble and go straight to performing.

Moving people and generating new configurations of people can be a powerful way to help people grow. Allowing people to experience different sorts of work and situations with a great team around them is the counterbalance and it is just as empowering and effective for the organisation.

Teams operated like this have time and space to plough learning back into the group. They can find amazing ways to solve problems for organisations. They can find even more amazing ways to create wealth for the organisation.

The ability and value of individuals involved in this type of team is amplified and enhanced. Organisations and companies who recognise this can reap an incredible return on the investment they have made in their people.

Historians who study societies have noticed certain tendencies. Societies that ignore outside influences and try to maintain internal power structures tend to stagnate. This applies to teams. You need your team and organisation to have a healthy regard for their environment. They need to be open to moving on and welcoming new members while retaining and fostering team identity and norms.

This applies to organisations. I believe it is also true of individuals. We need to open our windows and let in new influences and ideas.

Teams, managers and organisations who are confident in their abilities can get a lot of benefit from creating a learning environment and engaging in generative learning. By this I mean an environment where high quality feedback is encouraged. The feedback is used to generate a deep-level understanding of how the organisation works so that deep change can be engaged in. This requires commitment but gives a massive return on investment.

People making change understand

✔ Why they are making change.
✔ What that change is.
✔ How to make the right changes.
✔ What outcomes these changes should have.

The alternatives to understanding seem to include:

✗ Being at the mercy of external consultancy companies whose goal is to maximise their own profits by mass producing "one size fits all" solutions.
✗ Random initiatives based on what seems to be working for everyone else.
✗ Responding to symptoms rather than cause and avoiding the core issues.
✗ Being fearful of changing anything in case you break something.

Mostly when we talk about return on investment we are talking about return on money invested by the company in a course of action. We also want return on the investment of time and effort at a company, team and personal level.

As a manager you do not want to be running to stay still, or even worse, to catch up. You want to get the best possible return on investment for your management efforts.

Deep structure and balance

Imagine you are trying to balance two bags on a stick. You can't see what is in the bags. One is attached to a label that says 'toys' and the other is attached to a label that says 'tools'. The bags are swinging out of sight beneath your stick on long strings and they seem to be changing weight.

This is the situation you are in if you are trying to deal with just the surface structure of your life.

It all gets much easier if you can discover what exactly is in the bags and how much they weigh. It is even better if you have control over which things are taken from and which things are added to each bag. You can only get to this situation if you have a look at what is really inside the bags, not just the labels on your stick.

You must know what you are dealing with in order to achieve balance.

This is what it is to start understanding the deep structure of things. This is what it is to occupy a meta position based on principle and logic rather than being carried along by the forces of fashion, perception and the herd instinct for stampede or inertia.

It would be nice if things were 'either/or' choices. As a child this is how you think - for or against - either this or that. These are choices based on incomplete descriptions. As you get a handle on things as an adult, you realise that life is not like this at all.

The boundaries blur, even for things that once seemed to be clear cut. You regain the clarity and ability to make up your mind by finding out more, and by realising that the shades of grey between black and white are really just your growing ability to discern. This ability allows you to be more accurate about the point where black makes the crucial change on its journey to white. This is the balance point. This tells you the degree of balance and the latitude you have to play with.

The best place to start uncovering deep structure of a situation is to identify what you think you know. If you are mature enough you will take the old Chinese advice that the root of all wisdom is to admit ignorance.

Most of what we think we know is based on generalisations. It is also based on distortions caused by other people's perceptions, your attempts to match them with your own and in some cases by deliberate misinformation.

Finally there are things that you just do not know and might not even be aware that you do not know. These are deletions in your knowledge, blank spots in your map of what is going on.

Good, clear, thoughtful communication will help you to deal efficiently and effectively with most situations and prevent them from becoming problems.

We all have a deep structure. It is how we hold things in our brain and what we try to vocalise. The means of expressing this are faulty. We use words, figures of speech, non verbal communication and we think we can mind read.

The antidote is communication. Learn how to ask purposeful questions. Write down what you think you know and check it.

Write down what you need to know and find it out, deliberately.

Stay alert and attuned to imbalances that tell you that there is something you are not aware of and that you need to know. This works best when it becomes habit. The crucial skill is listening to what is really being said. Challenge yourself by asking yourself "How do I know that"?

Even if you express your understanding of your own deep structure well, you may not have been able to represent it accurately.

Even if you correctly represent your deep structure, others may connect what you have expressed to a different deep structure of their own.

This makes metaphor a vital communication skill.

Metaphor and meta-position

Kurt Gödel was probably one of the most important logicians of all time, although that can not be proven, nor would he have wanted it to be. He is most famous for two theorems known as the incompleteness theorems.

These are heavily based in the language of mathematics but to paraphrase them:

1 In any arithmetically sound axiom system, it is possible to construct true statements that are impossible to prove or disprove within the system.
2 The axioms that the systems are based on can not be proved or disproved by the system.

Within these I find two interestingly pertinent ideas:

- · The incompleteness of proof within any system.
- · Strange loops[57].

The incompleteness of proof states that if a system is consistent it cannot be complete. The consistency of the axioms cannot be proved within the system which is based on those same axioms.

I suppose you could say that you cannot use a ruler to measure itself.

This is very much more important than it sounds and makes a lot more sense than it seems to.

To explain what he meant:

"This statement can not be proven."

The top.
>   If the statement is false, it means the statement can be proved, which means it is true
>   However if it is true that it can not be proven, then that makes it proven, which makes it false.
Go back to the top

I am not a mathematician but I am still impressed by this. It came at a time when the mathematical world was declaring Euclidean mathematics to be the ultimate truth.

Many thought that all that was left for mathematics was to work through a lot of proofs. Gödel pointed out that proof and truth are not the same thing. They are not the same thing at

---

57 As proposed by Douglas Hofstadter in his book - Godel, Escher, Bach. There are strange loops in this book you are reading. Their relevance will be explained and explored in more detail in volume 2.

all; and that is a crucial philosophical idea that bleeds into everyone's life.

Gödel was, by all accounts, a towering intellect. People who talked to him felt as though he had already thought through any arguments they could possibly make.

Einstein said that it was a privilege to walk home with him from the Institute of Advanced study.

To me his theorems vastly simplified mean this: if you use the system which you are trying to validate, to produce the proof, then the proof is not complete.

1+1=2 can not be proved mathematically because mathematics hinges on the axiom that it is true. The proof has to come from another system. Mathematics is itself a metaphor and that makes 1+1=2 a metaphor for something you know about apples.

Even with mathematics you need to step out to a meta position. When mathematicians do this they see that there are different sorts of infinities and that there are true statements about numbers that can not be proved by the system.

If we were to apply this same sort of thinking to making change to an organisation or a process, would we see similarities here that lead to statements and axioms?

- If you are part of the system it is difficult to make a change.
- Making change is like negotiating.
- Making change is like problem solving.

You have to go into an abstract version of the systems and consider the axioms or assumptions upon which it is based.

Some people describe it as a super-consciousness, a meta-position, as though they can rise above it and see the connections outside of the current system or situation.

One way is to create a metaphor that joins the different systems of thinking. It may be that in our business world we have to balance the models of thinking. Different interpretations of the same words and events can mean different things to different people, so you need a way to negotiate a common starting point.

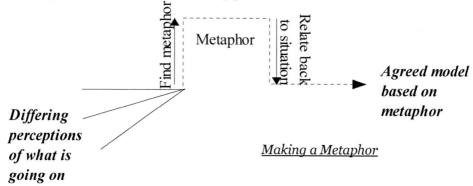

Differing perceptions of what is going on

Making a Metaphor

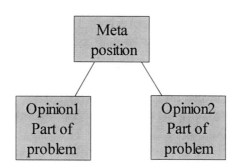

Viewing the Options

Balance

If you are part of the system, you are influenced by the system and you cannot be objective. You need someone who is not part of the problem, yet has the capacity to help you focus on what you are really trying to achieve. In order to break the deadlock they can take a meta position.

If you are in prison cell you are constrained by routine, your view of 4 walls and your fear of the warden.

Imagine if someone were to smuggle a trowel in for you. If you were to decide to tunnel out, you would first have to choose a direction to tunnel in or a wall to tunnel through. How do you do that when you have no idea of what is beyond your own four walls?

This is like the situation many managers have to deal with when they are constantly being drawn into daily politics and fire-fighting.

If you can get someone to give you a satellite image of the prison, you could start to see where you really are in relation to everyone else. More importantly you would start to see where you want to get to and what is the most direct and achievable route to get there.

When faced with impenetrable forests of process and routine it is a useful skill to be able to gain some height. It allows you to get a perspective on what is really going on. Someone once told me that the true leader is not the guy cutting the path through the forest with the machete. Look for the guy up the tree yelling "wrong forest" if you want a leader[58].

I went on holiday to a lovely little cottage. I used to get up every morning and spend over an hour cycling down the road

---

[58] Just make sure he is not a practical joker or a habitual forest changer!

to the lake for a swim. It was nice to have the lake so close by. The cycle was a tough one with lots of hills and I would arrive back from my swim quite dusty and sweaty, ready for another swim.

I had taken directions from the book of knowledge you find left at most rented gîtes. I had also consulted with one of the locals who confirmed this was the way to cycle to the lake. On my first trip to the nearby town I went to an internet café and looked up the region on Google Earth. I was amazed to see from the satellite image that the lake was no more than a few kilometres from the house as the crow flies.

On the strength of this I purchased an ordinance survey map and examined it that evening after tea for possibilities. I had indeed been taking the only route to the lake available by road the whole way, however there was a back road that went directly there but seemed to stop for a bit before joining the road to the lake.

The following morning I cycled the new route and found that it was full of potholes and that I had to carry the bike up a steep rocky trail between the roads for about 10 metres. It was my idea of a perfect cycle, no other traffic. The journey took no more than 20 minutes each way and I arrived back cheerfully refreshed from my swim.

I sketched a quick map showing the alternate route with a brief description in the book of knowledge. As I did so I thought of the seasons of morning swimmers who would think kindly of me when they read it and found my short-cut to the lake

Common mistake: Seeing things as you want them to be – not as they are. Although the map showed a road going directly there, I needed first hand experience, even after seeing a satellite image and a detailed map. Neither of them told me enough about the quality of the road or whether the gap between the roads was negotiable.

You need to see the possibilities but you also need to understand what influences and forces are at play. I had to take into account that I may have needed to turn around and cycle the usual way if the gap had been something impenetrable or private. I had to be willing to take that risk.

"One Truth" myth

In science we are apparently on the verge of a grand unifying theory of everything. In business we are nowhere near it.

I do understand the desire for there to be one truth which, once discovered, will never need to be changed again.

I have heard it from all sides of the political spectrum in business. I have heard it from practitioners of Agile methodologies, such as SCRUM, who declare it to be all you need. I have heard from practitioners of more traditional command and control methodologies, such as PRINCE2, who declare that their approach is perfection itself.

The principle I apply is this: The minute someone starts talking about "the only way" or "the one truth", it is time to start looking elsewhere. Exclusion is a dead end road.

I have seen SCRUM turning from a decent set of Agile principles into the ultimate command and control tool:
- If it is not on the backlog you can't even think about it.
- If you can't put a price on it, we are not doing it.
- The customer is always right.

Well the customer is not always right. Sometimes the

customer is very wrong and will not thank you for supporting them in their folly, no matter how many meetings you have with them.

I coached in a company that was trying out SCRUM. All the Project Managers had just been sent on SCRUM training courses. They came back and set up meetings with the customers and let the customer decide all the priorities.

This was all well and good, except for that fact that the customer was a proxy customer representing consumers. It turned out that he did not know his own consumer base as well as he thought he did.

The development team happened to contain consumers of the particular product. They understood better than the customer what his customers wanted. The developers actually knew his business better than he did.

It all turned out well. The developers were a pretty mature crew who convinced the customer that they really knew what they were doing.

They helped him make some tremendously good prioritisation and requirement decisions. They did this, not by pandering to his every wish, but by demonstrating that they were committed to producing the best product possible: a product they would use, themselves.

In some quarters Scrum has managed to declare that Agile is Scrum and that Scrum is Agile. Some practitioners maintain that it is all you need and the all other Agile methodologies are there to support Scrum. There is the faintest whiff that scrum is the one true faith.

Taylorism AKA Scientific Management

This was the brainchild of Frederick Winslow Taylor (1856-1915).

He studied things like optimal shovel sizes, shift duration and time and motion measurements.

To give him his due Taylor's stated outcomes were fairness and prosperity for the worker as well as generation of wealth for the capitalist system.

He proposed achieving this through:

✓ The development of the management of work as a real science.
✓ The scientific selection of workers.
✓ The scientific development of workers.
✓ Cooperation between management and workers.
✓ Equal division of work between management and workers.
✓ Each person doing the job to which they were best suited.

This actually led to:

✗ Authoritarianism
✗ Separation of planning from doing
✗ Temporary incentives
✗ Task specialisation
✗ Management detachment

Taylor believed there was a best way to do everything and set out to find it for every job in every company he worked for. I have seen claims that he was an obsessive compulsive who was compelled to measure absolutely everything in his life, which would explain a lot.

He was also acting in a historical context at the end of the 19th and beginning of the 20th centuries. He was part of a ferocious class system.

His ideas were hijacked to break unions, de-skill and undermine guilds, pay lower wages for more work and to sack and disenfranchise lots of workers.

Taylor spent a lot of time writing about the laziness of workers and the need to tell them what to do, how to do it and how long they had to do it in.

The mis-assumptions of the Taylorist philosophy are that:

✗ Maximising efficiency and profit are the main objectives for everyone involved and that the only measure is money.
✗ People will forsake everything to maximise income, including putting the organisation's goals and objective before their own happiness.
✗ Large growing companies are desirable in order to divide labour and create specialisation.

Taylor himself appears to have been bemused by the idea of anybody trying to use his techniques without also applying the philosophy of management collaboration and suiting people to the job.

Most everybody else in management, while they disliked Taylor himself, thought Taylorism was a great idea and it is still applied with varying levels of disaster by managers around the world.

Totalitarian regimes find Scientific Management particularly appealing. The Nazis used Scientific Management techniques for productivity in concentration camps.

Taylorism has been used to dehumanise work and to break the job down into smaller and smaller units in order to maximise productivity with nary a thought for job satisfaction.

As it is generally applied, it has the added draw, for megalomaniacs, of keeping workers ignorant, unskilled, isolated, dependant and highly suspicious of each other.

We must be careful of things like "Lean" and "SCRUM" which share the same stable as Taylorism. They too have tendencies toward "one best ways" and the maximisation of efficiency and profitability over all else. With a few philosophical adjustments or deletions they could end up being just as destructive to the lives of workers and industrial relations as Taylorism has been.

I am pleased to report that so far its thought leaders appear to be concerned with the human beings involved and with creating pleasant collaborative workplaces. Long may this be in the agenda.

The Consultant's Conundrum

I was talking to a fellow consultant working in another company. He was asking me about Agile. He wanted to know what it was all about. He asked me what I thought the main problem in the IT industry was. I gave him an answer that he confessed he had not expected and one which he felt inclined to agree with.

The problem is divide and conquer. Despite years of teaching otherwise on management courses many people still adhere to Taylorism as a system of management. It is as if the company is afraid of its own employees. It is the classic tug between fear and trust. In making sure its employees are kept under control they are willing to sacrifice all the benefits those people could bring to the company.

To this end they use process as a weapon. It is used to regulate and impede. In an effort to make this process efficient it is applied to everyone. Many processes I have seen have suffered because in an attempt to make the same thing work for everyone, everywhere. It is either incredibly complex, like PRINCE2, or it is incredibly generic and vague, like SCRUM.

If we take a company with an IT department they will probably have three very general divisions of interest.

 There will be the commercial aspect of the company. This will be various combinations of the people who are paying for, and/or using the software system.

There will be the development aspect that will be responsible for writing and maintaining the software system.

There will be the production aspect, responsible for the deployment and administration of the software system.

In many companies these departments see themselves as discrete entities with all the other departments as competition. Each department can have a set of objectives that are mutually exclusive to the objectives of the other departments.

There is a big difference in the way companies tend to behave depending on their size.

Large companies are like continents with each department becoming a country state. The states are vying with each other for federal budget allocations. There are spin doctors, ambassadors, legislative assemblies, generals and local dictators.

There are sometimes even a few departments trying to secede from the union. It most amusing to watch attempts at industrial espionage and sabotage within the same alleged corporate entity.

Smaller companies tend to be like ships on the ocean. The lines of communication are shorter. People are aware they are sharing a fate.

This tends to lead people to concentrate on their own lifeboat. Real effort has to be put in to prevent the communication from becoming disjointed. The captain has to be adept at multi-tasking to ensure the engine room is getting the right messages. The divide between Development and Production is not so great because they tend to be the same people.

In the small software companies I have worked for, Production and Support has depended on the size of the customer. Small customers rely heavily on the suppliers of the software to provide this service. Larger customers train up their own people to do this job. They only approach the supplier with exceptional support issues.

In every sort of company, regardless of size, there is a tension between commercial, support and development. It may manifest itself in different ways, but it is always there.

None of these conceptual players can exist for long without the others. The basic question is where to put the emphasis, how much and for how long? The basic answer is to make all these tribes realise that their fates are intertwined. They may have very different concerns, interim outcomes and modus operandi but if they go to war they will all lose, regardless of the outcomes of the battles. Much like real war.

Understanding the consultant's conundrum

Having discussed some of this, the consultant confessed to me that he had a bit of a conundrum.

At his company the developers' performance was being measured by how many features they could add to the system. The production team's performance was being measured by the stability of the system.

The developers were using an Agile methodology which meant that they wanted to deliver features to production every two weeks. Production saw this as a huge threat to the stability of the system they were being paid to protect. They were using a waterfall[59] methodology to make sure that all change was tied up with red tape until rendered safe.

The result was a huge headache for the IT manager and the consultant who had been called in to help sort it out. They were searching for a methodology which would cover the concerns of all the departments without changing their targets.

From a commercial point of view both sets of measures made sense. They wanted the new features in the system which allowed them to sell services. They also wanted their system to be stable.

The developers were being rewarded and awarded bonuses on progress against the requirements list. The production team was being rewarded and awarded bonuses on the basis of stability of the system.

Naturally the developers and project managers wanted the new features introduced into the live system. Equally

---

59 Waterfall is a term used to describe a model in which development is seen as progressing through a series separate phases: Requirements, design, implementation, verification and maintenance. Each of the phases has a one way gate and the next is not started until the current one is completed. Winston Royce presented it in 1970 as an example of a non working model. Its use has been widespread in Software Development and requires Big Design Up Front (BDUF). The argument is that it is a measure twice cut once approach. Unfortunately is it not suited to the fast changing world of software development. Rather than prevent costly mistakes by getting the design right, it introduces flawed thinking and creates obstructions to mistakes being rectified at all.

naturally the production team and their managers considered new features to be a risk they needed to constrain.

Both sets of people were acting rationally on the basis of both self interest and professional responsibility. They had been encouraged to view the other department as rivals. This rivalry was creating an impasse which was upsetting people.

The consultant had been asked to come up with a methodology and an approach that would resolve this. He was trying to decide between Agile and waterfall. He was searching for an all-encompassing methodology that would satisfy both camps and he was at his wits end.

Bonuses and rosettes

Not only was he searching for the one true methodology but he was hobbled by the commonly held assumption that competition creates excellence. This is an example of truth and proof being different things.

In my experience excellence is achieved in spite of competition not because of it. The existence of both things side by side does not mean there is a causal relationship between them.

Competition creates blinkered idiots who see the world through the prism of their bonus. If you are in competition with someone for a limited bonus pot, why on earth would you help them?

Excellence is derived from hard work guided by collaboration and creativity. Collaboration and creativity are stifled by competition.

This runs deeper than interdepartmental competition. The

bonus culture creates inter-team competition and even competition between the members of the same team.

To this end personal objectives are maintained over team objectives and self interest is levered as if it were the only reason anyone would ever do anything.

The theory is that if you have enough control you can give people individual targets and motivate and reward them with bonus payments.

Only the fat controller[60] needs to know the grand objective. All the little objectives added up are supposed create the big objective. This is the sort of reductionist nonsense that is bringing our economy to its knees.

Myth of the one true methodology

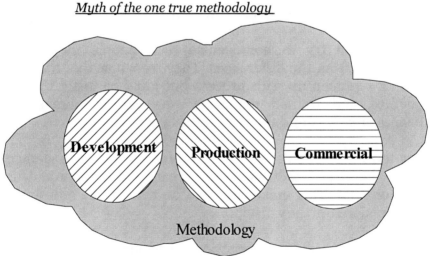

Imagine employing a team of talented artists. To be sure that they do not paint anything you do not like, you make them use paint-by-numbers kits. When the artists get incredibly bored some of them start to do sloppy work. Some of them

---

60 Thomas the Tank Engine

just paint all the squares blue to comply with productivity targets. They finish lots of kits to get their bonus.

Do you clap yourself on the back at being right about not trusting them or do you admit that there might be a better way to manage skilled professionals?

So much potential is paid for by companies and then wasted because the companies are afraid of the power of that potential. In many cases the very skills and talents they spend a fortune on inhibiting are the ones that the company needs in order to succeed.

Advantage from the interactions of difference

Successful companies and teams I have encountered do quite the opposite. They encourage their employees to use the full range of skills and experience at their disposal.

Rather than try to homogenise their people they create advantage from the differences. They recognise that the slack cannot be taken up with process but must be taken up with talented and trained managers who can encourage and inspire creativity and focus it on the task at hand.

Far too many people are being promoted into management roles because tradition has created a "them-and-us" environment. This makes management seem like a desirable progression from any discipline.

Management is a specialised discipline and requires specialised training and experience. It is not a progression from anything except management. If management were seen as part of the team, and progression towards excellence within other disciplines were to be rewarded equally well, things would improve vastly.

That management is seen as a superior role is a misunderstanding of the function of hierarchy. Some people's talents and preferences lead them to management roles. Some people are inspired to make things.

Risk Related Pay

I am tired of hearing senior executives of companies claiming that the risks they take justify the obscene salaries they command. Unless they own the company, and that is another story, they are taking risks with someone else's money.

I observe the guys who collect the bins every week taking far greater personal risks with what some people leave in their trash. Yet they are not paid for risk. They are paid on the premise that collecting bins is a horrible job and only people who have no choice will do it. Therefore they can be paid subsistence.

Imagine the effect if the top three levels of management in all the major companies were to disappear overnight. The companies would keep producing and many of us would see no difference.

Now imagine if all the bin men in the country were to stop working.

Bonuses

Management is an essential function but it needs to regain balance.
- A good manager is not a boss.
- A good manager does not need to conceal the big picture in order to keep a weather eye on it.
- Because they have responsibility for the big picture does not mean they own it nor does it mean that they need to carry it

alone.

In my experience managers who share the big objectives with their colleagues[61] are more likely to achieve them. It also forces them to have an objective to share, other than that of getting their bonus by hook or by crook.

Profit sharing bonuses, rather than individual bonuses, create better results. This is because people who are not vying with each other for a pot of money tend to cooperate more. They are prepared to consider more win-win solutions.

Foundation

Isaac Asimov's Foundation trilogy tells a story where the future has been mathematically predicted. Once it can be predicted it can be manipulated.

It is the story of a colony of people who are aware that there is a grand plan which must not be upset in case of dire consequences.

Essential intervention points exist on the plan. These must be observed and managed with care in order to avoid a great catastrophe.

The twist in the tail is that much has been concealed. The revelations and predictions, that they are trusting to guide them, conceal a hidden agenda. If they were to know the true nature of the future, the variables in their behaviour would become too unpredictable.

The story works because Asimov manages to convince us that it is plausible that his character, the mathematician Hari Seldon, can actually mathematically predict the future.

---

61 The people you manage are your colleagues.

He also admits that even the great Hari Seldon can only predict general trends. He can not foresee the effect of extraordinary individuals.

This is science fiction fantasy.

The future is unpredictable.

In business this has never been a more relevant principle. We need people who can roll with the punches. We need people who can collaborate without the need for cosseting or micromanagement. Companies need to realise that controlling people and trying to second guess such a chaotic system as the Market, is a wasteful and futile sap on resource.

Investing in people who can ride the Zeitgeist and rise to the challenge should be more than something you say as a sound-bite to attract graduates. People really are your most valuable resource. People who have resources and balance as they surf and rise, without the need for a handler, are the most valuable.

More and more companies are demanding exhibitions of company dependence and single mindedness. This creates company drones.

Now is a time when we really need people who have already found balance between professional excellence and personal independence. These are people whose outlook on life and work allows them to maintain poise and balance atop a great swell of change.

A good friend once described it as the ability to tap dance on a landslide.

Some Advice on the Consultant's Conundrum

Here is what I specifically counselled my fellow consultant: ***Identify the unique and the shared. Integrate the organisation.***

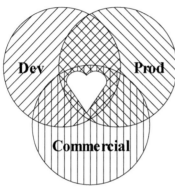

✔ Look for the things that all the departments currently agree on.

✔ Identify things they do in common, even if they call them by different names

Step 1 - <u>Identify the Shared</u>

✔ Cooperation in these will lead to more areas of commonality and agreement once people start to discover common objectives.

✔ Encourage them to recognise the value in other departments' concerns and then to find ways to accommodate other departments' goals.

✔ ***New ways of working will emerge: nurture them!***

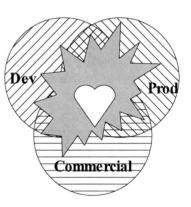

Step 2 - <u>Build on the Shared</u>

✔ Encourage them to identify and to cut out unnecessary process and procedure.

✔ This should get easier for them as they start trusting the other areas they interact with. They will find that complimentary behaviours from colleagues support their own objectives.

Step 3 - <u>Identify the Unique</u>

✔ In time, what is necessarily unique to a department will shrink.

✔ Pragmatically there will always be special cases. It is more effective to treat these as special cases.

Step 4 - <u>Refine</u>

Organisational Parts Integration

Step 1:
Identify the shared

Step 2:
Expand the
shared

Step 3:
Identify the Unique

Step 4:
Refine:
Discard the
unnecessary

Management support

W Edwards Deming had a list of things that he considered golden rules. The first and foremost among these had to do with management. He firmly believed that if there is a problem it can always, always, always be traced back to the management of a company[62].

The glorious flip side of this is the realisation that the solution to a problem can also be initiated by the management of a company. If problems permeate downwards, then so too does good leadership and innovation.

Innovation is born of flexibility of thought and execution.

Here are some ideas based on my observations of great managers:

- Flexibility of approach.
  - → A willingness to change the methodology
- *The methodology should be recursive and fractal.*
  - → A constant examination of the process to ensure that it is supporting the outcomes and objectives which are

---

62 "Out of the Crisis" by W. Edwards Deming.

themselves constantly reviewed.

- Flexibility of management.
  - → The first law of cybernetics can be interpreted that the most flexible component in a system is the most valuable. In this human system a flexibility of management approach makes it tremendously valuable.
- Managers as enablers.
  - → There is a misconception that people have to comply with management. The converse is the only way management can work effectively. Management is there to take responsibility and to direct. It must comply with the needs of the managed.
- Allow people to flourish in the areas where they excel and where they are happy.
  - → Enable salary and recognition progression in all disciplines. This should be earned through experience and skill. Learning and master-craftsmanship should be rewarded.
- Preventing problems is a far more valuable and cost effective skill than solving them.
  - → Notice people who are rarely if ever in the limelight of damage control.
- Managers should be encouraged to change their focus from control to support.
  - → Reviews and progress meetings can be perceived as an opportunity for a manager to discover how to make the job a better fit for the employee in order to encourage productivity.

Use the people you have.

There is no point wishing you had people other than you do. Many companies find that they trade one set of people for another and still have the same problems.

I have seen people who had been consigned to the scrap heap becoming star players after receiving a bit of genuine encouragement through the application of skilled coaching.

Find ways to utilise the people you have and recognise their training, experience, skills, and knowledge. Allow them to change and this change will be beneficial to the company.

You can not force change or compliance if you want flexibility. Change must come through coaching, training and communication.

Balance flexibility and stability

There will always be a tension between stability and flexibility. Bind them together with an unbreakable wire. On the wire that joins them you must make sure that you know where you want to be.

Is your business one which needs to respond to changes in a fluid and aggressive market or are you offering your customers some sort of product whose value is in its unchanging nature?

It pays to be aware that this balance may change from team to team, project to project or iteration to iteration.

Decide where your company sits for this project. Be prepared

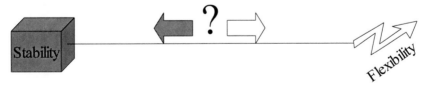

yourself and prepare all the players. You may need to move either way along this line on a case by case basis.

Fractal Balance and recursion

The methodology is there to support the main function of the business and, to that end, it needs to be flexible, recursive and fractal. People need to be flexible. The product does not always need to be. You must make that distinction.

- Avoid company wide dictates which attempt to impose one size fits all solutions. These force people into unproductive behaviours. They attempt to conform to the dictate rather than address challenges or realise opportunities.
- Encourage flexible thinking which produces cost effective and profitable solutions to the problems in hand and creates opportunities from them.

Balance is fractal and that is a good thing. You balance the big things on either side of the equation. Then you balance the things that make up these. Then balance the things inside those and inside those as necessary.

Fractal Balance

In the example of the consultant's conundrum, Developers and Operations staff need to be encouraged to identify which parts of the system give most benefit from being changeable. They need to identify the parts for which there is no business benefit in being flexible. They need to understand risk and benefit.

Balance

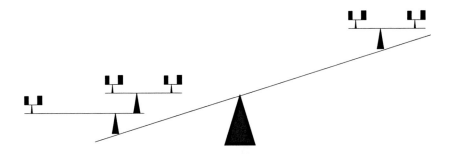

<u>*Efficient Fractal Imbalance*</u>

Doing the wrong thing well. Efficient but ineffective. Arranging deckchairs on the Titanic. Local optimisations. All the details are sorted out but not the main objective.

The overall balance must take precedence over local optimisations.

You can afford to have inefficiencies as long as the overall balance is maintained.

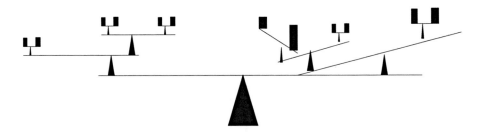

<u>*Effective Fractal Imbalance*</u>

Doing the right thing but with room for improvement: Effective with room for efficiencies. There is overall Balance but some work remains on the details.

In seeking efficiency and implementing change, be sure you maintain the overall balance. It is more important than whatever gains you might make locally.

181

A flexible approach will maintain an overall balance and be able to cope with detailed balancing as it becomes necessary.

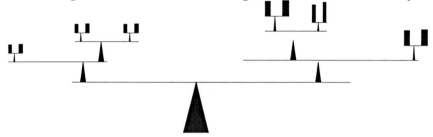

Total Fractal Balance
Doing the right thing well: Effective and highly efficient. There is overall balance and all the details are sorted out.

Change agents

In order to create and maintain balance you must be able to change things. If you are trying to change things you must be able to move them about.

If you wish to change the way in which a department or an entire organisation operates, you will need to employ a change agent.

This person must be trained in Systems Thinking. Their goal should be the improvement of working practices to facilitate the main business function of the company.

If the change agent favours a particular approach then you need to be sure that their advice is based on the particular needs of your organisation rather than the promotion of their own career.

Someone who is truly committed to the advancement of the company will readily tell you the limitations of their proposed approach.

If you are serious about change and you want your change agents to be effective, here are some things you need to consider:

✔ Change agents need to have reasonable authority[63]. They can not be restricted by the system they are trying to change (see section on incompleteness theorem).

✔ Change is an ongoing process vital to the survival of the company. Change agents should have the very highest priority in terms of resource deployment and recruitment.

✔ Change will be most effective if all agendas are out in the open. To this end there should be an open and honest relationship with the directorship of the company.

✔ Change can not be introduced by trickery or stealth. It requires openness and honesty within the entire organisation.

✔ The cost and impact of change must be discussed realistically. Senior management wilfully believing in the tooth fairy is a sackable offence in my book.

✔ Change agents must be people capable of seeing all sides when looking at the bigger picture. A common mistake is to exclude all detail and call what is left the big picture. Some details are essential to the understanding of the big picture.

✔ These people need to be comfortable with detail and with

---

63 W. Edwards Deming, one of the most successful change agents in business, would not consider any offers of work unless he was approached personally by the managing director and given certain guarantees.

overviews. They must be able to flow seamlessly between them.

✔ They must know what life is like for the people into whose life they are introducing change.

✔ Overall, they need to be able to communicate with the different sorts of people who make up your organisation. They should frame objectives and ideas for their audiences. They must be able to balance the needs of the individuals with the needs of the group.

On balance I would have to say...Jazz

Have you ever listened to good jazz? Jazz is a wide categorisation but all really good jazz has one thing that makes it different: Truly good jazz is played by great musicians and it is played without a net.

Miles Davis' album "Kind of Blue" is the best selling jazz record ever. On the sleeve notes Bill Evans[64] writes that when the players arrived, Miles gave them the briefest sketch then set off recording.

What you hear on this amazing album is the first complete performance of each piece. One of the musicians compared the experience to following Miles out onto a tightrope.

The musicians have no written music and rely on their ability to balance what they are playing with what they are hearing around them. If you were to sit in on the session and write it all down and then ask the same or another group of musicians to play it, there would be something missing. It would not be jazz. Jazz does not lend itself well to reductionism.

In the same sleeve notes Bill Evans writes "**Aside from the weighty technical problem of collective coherent thinking, there is the very human, even social need for sympathy from all members to bend for the common result.**"

The ability to play jazz relies on the ability to improvise. Improvising means knowing what to do that will fit the current reality and maintain the balance. It generally requires a great deal of skill and experience. It comes from knowing what is essential and when it is essential. The sleeve notes

---

64 http://www.billevanswebpages.com/kindblue.html

comment on this too "**Miles Davis presents here frameworks which are exquisite in their simplicity and yet contain all that is necessary to stimulate performance with sure reference to the primary conception.**".

Jazz is as rewarding to play as it is to listen to. It involves the listener with the players. Jazz is what classical musicians play on their own time.

This ***controlled freedom*** applies to many things in life. This ability to balance on a tightrope comes in the muscle training and produces more than the sum of its parts.

Context

"Now, Watson, confess yourself utterly taken aback," said he.

"I am."

"I ought to make you sign a paper to that effect."

"Why?"

"Because in five minutes you will say that it is all so absurdly simple."

"I am sure that I shall say nothing of the kind."

"You see, my dear Watson,"—he propped his test-tube in the rack, and began to lecture with the air of a professor addressing his class —"it is not really difficult to construct a series of inferences, each dependent upon its predecessor and each simple in itself. If, after doing so, one simply knocks out all the central inferences and presents one's audience with the starting-point and the conclusion, one may produce a startling, though possibly a meretricious, effect. Now, it was not really difficult, by an inspection of the groove between your left forefinger and thumb, to feel sure that you did NOT propose to invest your small capital in the gold fields."

"I see no connection."

"Very likely not; but I can quickly show you a close connection. Here are the missing links of the very simple chain:

1. You had chalk between your left finger and thumb when you returned from the club last night.

2. You put chalk there when you play billiards, to steady the cue.

3. You never play billiards except with Thurston.

4. You told me, four weeks ago, that Thurston had an option on some South African property which would expire in a month, and which he desired you to share with him.

5. Your check book is locked in my drawer, and you have not asked for the key.

6. You do not propose to invest your money in this manner."

"How absurdly simple!" I cried.

"Quite so!" said he, a little nettled. "Every problem becomes very childish when once it is explained to you. ..."

From The Return of Sherlock Holmes
(The Adventure of the Dancing Men)
- Sir Arthur Conan Doyle

187

Context, pretext and plain text

Most of us like a good mystery. Since Wilkie Collins wrote the Moonstone, which is widely attributed to be the first detective novel, we have loved the idea of the detective. The detective is a person who can notice detail that no one else notices or who can make inferences from detail that every one else has missed. Usually this detail or inference spins the context on its head and a new explanation of events unravels. The murderer is caught, the jewels were in the sugar all the time or there was never any crime at all.

What did Sherlock do on the previous page? What allowed him to amaze Watson? Why, when it was explained, was Watson as underwhelmed as Holmes predicted he would be?

Watson started out seeing the situation in one context. From that context it appeared that what Holmes had done was impossible.

When Holmes changed his context for him, it became absurdly simple. "Impossible" to "Absurdly simple" in a single leap. Was it the detail or the big picture that Holmes presented that provided the illumination? We shall see.

In recent years television has enabled a new type of time dilated story telling. Story arcs are all the rage. Clever writers of series such as "Lost" tell us stories. We set off with them, thinking we know with whom we sympathise and for whom we reserve our loathing.

From week to week they reveal details. They have the luxury of flashback, flash forward and flash sideways. They introduce new characters, revelations and situations into what we thought we knew.

Context

Nothing which has gone before is invalidated, and this is the part we should really admire. With all the revelations and context switches the story stays internally consistent.

We are forced to reappraise what we have seen and reassess the nature of our heroes and villains. We run back through the events we have witnessed, we see events and actions from a different perspective and the story takes on new meanings and implications.

Have you ever found yourself in a situation which seemed intractable? Have you ever had to solve an apparently impossible problem? What happened?

Think of a time when you felt that you were faced with the impossible. Whatever happened then you are here now reading this book. Your life continued. It must have resolved things in some way.

Were you happy with the outcome? Did you have a flash of insight or did something else change? What allowed you to make a decision or to take action? When you think of it now how does it compare to how it looked when you were in the middle of it?

Listen and see how we get to grips with this.

Mostly we find ourselves in impossible situations because we have trapped ourselves in a context. The ability to change the context and to change the perspective is the crucial move that lets us resolve these situations. Even doing nothing will force a resolution because if we do not change the context, the context changes us.

What happens when we can not make a decision in a context where all actions seem to lead to disaster or to undesired outcomes?

There is certainly a delay if we deploy an inspector Lestrade[65] to support the status quo. We start rationalising and the problem is simply commuted temporarily. Sooner or later we will have to face it and it will probably have turned from an opportunistic problem into a serial one.

If, on the other hand, we keep Lestrade tied up with paperwork, our natural ability to switch context kicks in. Our inner detective gets to work.

If we let this Sherlock off the leash he presents us with a report some time later. This report usually contains some detail that we thought we had not noticed or some clue that cracks the case wide open.

The best way to employ this detective is to present him with what you know and a clear list of your priorities in this case. It is best to then get out of the detective's way and go for a mental walk. Perhaps you could take a literal walk or go home for the evening.

When you have almost forgotten the case you will get a metaphorical tap on the shoulder and Sherlock will eagerly demonstrate his powers of observation and deduction - Elementary.

After the detective has solved enough cases your inner Lestrade will forget about being obstinate and come to respect and learn from him.

---

65 Inspector Lestrade is the "shockingly conventional" Scotland Yard detective who appears in the Sherlock Holmes stories. He does not understand or approve of Holmes' methods but takes public credit for the successes they provide. Holmes is quite fond of him and over time Lestrade comes to trust and admire Holmes and even learn from him.

Context

"We're not jealous of you down at Scotland Yard. No, sir, we are damned proud of you, and if you come down to-morrow there's not a man, from the oldest inspector to the youngest constable, who wouldn't be glad to shake you by the hand."

Inspector Lestrade speaking in
The Return of Sherlock Holmes
(The Adventure of the Six Napoleons)
- Sir Arthur Conan Doyle

Sometimes, even in the most successful cases Holmes needed to rethink his strategy and discard what he thought he knew. He realised that he had been looking at the whole thing from the wrong perspective. He had been relying on false assumptions about the mystery to be solved.

In the story, he has analysed the evidence and is concentrating his powers on a solution, but just as he is about to get to grips there is a disconnect. Something just does not fit. He re-examines the evidence, interviews different witnesses and, most of all, pursues a different line of questioning.

A different interpretation of events comes to light. The real mystery is uncovered. Now that he is pursuing the right mystery and he is unstoppable.

We need to be aware of our own detective's instinct and respond to it. An impasse may just be that we have been pursuing the wrong line of questioning. It may be that we have uncovered the Red Herring.

A context switch is forced on you sooner or later by events, so you might as well stay in control and switch context voluntarily.

In business the question "How can we deliver this in time?" can very quickly change to "What does not delivering this on time mean? How are we going to keep this client's business?".

If you keep trying to deliver something on time when it is clear you can't, you will lose the business if you do not move up a level and consider this really important question.

When you find yourself really struggling to define or agree on what you want, you may need to ask yourself: "Do we need or want anything like this at all?".

I have spent a lot of time with clients who are trying to specify the requirement for computer systems and they quite often just need to be reminded of the purpose of the system. This can result in many features, which had been causing raised blood pressure, dropping off the priority list altogether.

When you find yourself trying to decide between two options with no way to decide between them, it may help to ask "Does it make any difference at all which choice I make?". It may not, so you can close your eyes, point and get on with something that does make a difference!

Neither "either", nor "or"

In the section, entitled "The Map", when talking about methodologies and meta rules, we saw that we are often being sold a lie when we are presented with "*either/or*" decisions. The way out of this lie is the ability to manage context.

When many people consider context they imagine it to be yet another "*either/or*" choice.

The greatest managers, the greatest teachers and the greatest friends I have are people who can keep several contexts the table at the same time. Furthermore they can see the relationship between the contexts, just like Mr Sherlock Holmes above. They can see the sequence between the details and the big picture.

They have the picture from the lid of the jigsaw box and they can analyse the shapes of the pieces. They see where the sky goes and they can fit the almost identical blue bits together effectively and efficiently.

In order to balance something you must know what sort of weights you are dealing with. Are you balancing tonnes or microgrammes?

Context in the trousers of reality

If you remember I told you at the outset about my brother and the wrong leg of the trousers on the map and how this led directly to discovery that all decisions are actually a negotiation of the trousers of reality.

The biggest single problem I have to help people solve is the one of context. I start by helping them to understand the relationship between hierarchy, scope and context. Many people get in a blue funk arguing about details. This is a clear sign they have gone down the wrong leg of the trousers of reality.

Let me put it like this. If you are having problems with the details and if everyone is getting hot under the collar about trivia, then you might as well have a neon sign screaming "Stop! Go back!".

Have you heard the expression that if you do not know whether you have been in love or not, then you haven't been? Well if you are arguing about details rather than discussing them, they don't matter. What does matter is that something at the previous level of detail needs to be fixed. In this situation arguing about details is like trying to fix the tracks under a moving train.

You may be on the wrong track or you may be riding the wrong train on the right track. You can get back on the right track for this journey by examining the decision that got you here.

You can get back in the right train for this track by reappraising your outcomes for this course of action. Either way, you need to follow the context back up the hierarchy and fix it immediately.

Many details that people argue about become contentious because they are out of scope. People have assumed levels of decision that have not been made yet. They jump ahead. In difficult cases they are trying to force the decision by focussing everyone on the decisions down the particular leg they are in favour of. Once you engage in this with them you drag everyone down that leg by default.

You lose perspective if you engage in this, because now everyone is down this leg and you are left trying to describe what is down the other leg. What is down the other leg is now obscured by the detail of this leg. The path of power is back up the trousers until you can see back down both legs again.

It may be one person or the whole group that has become derailed. You are arguing about the details because you have lost the flow as a group. You need to get back and make sure everyone has come with you.

One sure-fire way to do this is to focus everyone on the outcomes at the highest level and decide how you will know when you have achieved them. When this has been decided then you can work backwards and create an outcome-focussed plan. This type of planning tends to focus on the right level of detail.

It is not enough to do it right, you must **do the right thing**. If you are doing the right thing, then doing it right will be self supporting. Details will be easier to negotiate.

For success you must be able to keep both of these contexts in your peripheral vision at all times. You must be able to negotiate the hierarchy.

Hierarchy is an onion (part 1)

- Context
- Focus
- Scope
- Frame
- Hierarchy
- Layers

We use all of these words and more to try to explain a phenomenon that lies at the heart of the cognitive process. It is something we do very well. We do it so well that we trap ourselves in it. I have already discussed the temporal, syntactical, spatial, semantic and collective constructs we use to create oases of stability in the shifting maelstrom of reality. I referred to them as pitons in the wall of reality. They were:

- *The perception, naming and measurement of time.*
- *Categories and taxonomies of entities and groups.*
- *Financial and economic structures.*
- *Social and professional organisations.*
- *Political and geographical borders.*
- *Career and entitlements.*
- *Age, nationality, status, membership and qualifications.*

In short the boundaries and distinctions we choose to recognise.

These are metaphors. These are stepping stones. Their strength is that they are not reality. The strength of a "software" system is that it is a metaphor that can be changed. It does not need to be reality. It can not be reality. The same applies to maps, plans and language itself.

The oasis is a mirage. It has arbitrary boundaries. If we lose sight of that simple fact, then what was put down as a temporary place-holder becomes confused with the place itself.

We can find ourselves detached from the centre, out of balance and out of context, holding a false centre. Like a tightrope walker who does not know where his centre of balance is any more, we think that the next raise or shiny toy will stabilise our pendulum.

We are at our best when we can distinguish the map from the territory, the plan from the event, the software from the system, the organisation from the people, the metaphor from the object.

An onion has layers. Each of the layers is essential to the onion being an onion. The core is the core for all of the onion. The skin is the skin for all of the onion.

Each layer lies as the skin or the core to the layers on either side of it. The closer you come to the centre the closer you come to the heart of the onion. The centre is the seed of the onion. The centre is the purpose[66].

---

66 An onion actually grows from centre of the base. This still holds for the metaphor but it is neater if we take poetic licence and imagine a seed at the centre.

We talk of core business, core values, core activities, core personnel and core practices all the time in business.

With the onion as our metaphor we need to decide whether these core things are the result of reductionism or refinement. At the core do we have brown rotting matter deprived of the nutrients of common sense or do we have the beating heart of innovation and clear purity of purpose?

Purity

Purity has become a much maligned concept due in great measure to the legacy of the 16th century puritans. When I talk about purity in this book I have a good idea that their version is not what you or I want to be associated with.

I wonder if you can think of any experience now you have had in your life that you would categorise as pure? Here are some of the things I associate with purity:

- A sip of Rare Irish Whiskey.
- A cheese sandwich in a café beside the Seine.
- Holding my daughter for the first time.
- The music of Chopin.
- Hearing a nightingale in my garden on a summers evening.
- Plunging into the sea aged 12.
- The paintings of Vermeer.
- Fred Astair and Ginger Rogers.
- Baryshnikov dancing.
- Jussi Bjorling's voice.
- The opening bars of a Beethoven symphony in a packed concert hall.

It does not matter whether we agree on these specific things. I am sure you have your own list.

Do you have some memory of something you could put in this category, which even now brings a shiver of pleasure to your spine when you think of it?

For many of us this is likely to be some experience that was entirely and totally what it was. It is usually something distilled to its essence like my Irish whiskey.

Irish whiskey is distilled three times. This is the law in Ireland. Technically it has practically no impurities left. It glides down the throat and you are advised to only sip, savouring each mouthful.

It can be argued that at times it is the impurities that make some things interesting. When I was learning how to make effective presentations I had to practice talking and giving a presentation without any body movement at all. I had to learn to use just my voice.

It was incredibly difficult at first. I kept waving my hands without any awareness that I was doing it. It took honest feedback from my coach and an effort of will to achieve stillness. It took practice to make it effortless.

From the stillness it was easier to add meaningful gestures and movements.

If we strip something back to its basics we can appreciate the impact and the value of what is added. We can see what is essential and what is optional. Knowing what is optional gives us choice, control and appreciation.

Zen and the art of context

Have you ever read "Zen and the Art of Motorcycle Maintenance" by Robert M Pirsig? I read it years ago when I was about 16. It had a profound effect on my sixteen year old self. It is largely a discussion of the nature of quality. It is also about people who see the world in terms of gestalt[67] and those who see it in terms of detail.

What I remember most was his description of stripping down a motorcycle motor. He describes laying the parts down on the ground in the order in which they are taken off the bike. That way he knew the order in which to reassemble the motor.

It is 30 years since I read that book but I still recall where I was and what I was thinking as I read that description. It influenced the way I approached problems from then on.

The ability to move between the gestalt and the detail is a way to unfetter the thought process. It forces one to recognise both reductionist and holistic views of the world and to understand when and why context forces one or the other.

If you do not control your context it will control you.

Refinement as a language

As a software engineer I noticed that things that take a round trip have their impurities or defects exposed. Moving to another context and back again enables an observer to understand and remove ambiguities and errors. It can be an effective way to approach testing.

---

67 A gestalt view is one that things are different than the sum of their parts. The German word means shape or form. It is also a school of psychology founded in 1912.

Context

Take an on-line translator[68] from English to French for example:

- Type in a fairly complex sentence.
- Translate it from English to French.
- Translate the result back from French to English,
- Translate the result of that again from English to French,
- Translate the result back again from French to English.
- Compare the initial sentence with the resulting sentence.

- **I hear you will be visiting next Friday**
- *J'entends dire que vous visiterez vendredi prochain*
- **I hear that you will visit next Friday**
- *J'entends dire que vous visiterez vendredi prochain*
- **I hear that you will visit next Friday**

You will notice that the English sentence was changed by the translator on the round trip, a middle ground was found that preserved the meaning. From this change, stability was achieved.

Now let's try something with more difficulty built in:

- **I hear that you will visit next Friday and that you will let me have a loan of your headphones and that you will have a lead for me jobwise.**
- *J'entends dire que vous visiterez vendredi prochain et que vous me permettrez d'avoir un prêt de votre casque et que vous aurez une avance pour moi jobwise.*
- **I hear that you will visit next Friday and that you will allow me to have a loan of your helmet and that you will have an advance as me jobwise.**

---

68 I used http://translation2.paralink.com/ which was the first one that came up on google.

- *J'entends dire que vous visiterez vendredi prochain et que vous me permettrez d'avoir un prêt de votre casque et que vous aurez une avance pour moi jobwise.*
- I hear that you will visit next Friday and that you will allow me to have a loan of your helmet and that you will have an advance as me jobwise.

Notice that the mistakes in the sentence are magnified by the round trip in translation. The escalating error is a clarification that something is wrong. It highlights what is wrong and it directs us to where it is wrong.

In a real situation, what might be a subtle, unnoticed error is made large enough to see and fix.

In the example there is a problem with the translation of "headphones". Notice also that there is an attempt in this (surprisingly good) translation program to balance the mistake. When it reaches a state of balance it continues to translate the same thing backwards and forwards without any more change.

I use this sort of testing strategy in testing software, particularly where data processing is going on. I pass the same data both ways through the system, checking for differences and passing the processed data back through the system more than once.

This approach results in the sort of refinement that not only fixes errors but which also simplifies and focuses the code.

It has a number of effects:

- Any errors will be magnified on the third pass as above.
- In fixing the process errors
    - → false assumptions about the data are revealed
    - → the process is almost always simplified
    - → the absolute requirements are clarified

This is because of two things

1. Inbuilt short feedback loops
2. The necessity to identify and excise the unnecessary.

One of the very earliest ways we learn to design systems is to:

- Analyse the existing physical system.
- Represent the physical system as a purely logical system.
- Refine the logical representation to remove constraints and inefficiencies.
- Translate the logical back to the physical again.

In practice, any but the simplest systems have to take this round trip a number of times in order to get a decent design. It is closely linked with the idea of evolution. What is strong and true in the design survives.

I have worked with systems designers who are only concerned with the quality of the logical design. They miss this crucial and useful process of iteration.

Through iteration you learn how physical implementation is going to treat your design. If you are aware of it, this is where your design starts to be perfected.

If they have isolated themselves from the context of

implementation, they have no idea how many requirements will need to be added, deleted and changed once the system leaves the drawing board in order for it to actually work. Thus assumptions are made.

Many designs seem to be perfectly fine until someone tries to implement them. It is only then that the disconnect between the theory and the reality comes to light.

The developers see this and put in workarounds to try to make the physical system function. In this way the logical and the physical start to diverge.

The design needs the journey through the forge of implementation in order to be refined. What is needed is collaboration between the designers and developers. It requires feedback close to the action, in short loops. There are those who say that those who design the system should have to implement their designs in order to learn how to design.

In many organisations the designers and the developers have very different maps of reality. When they do share a map, things start to improve for everyone immediately. When management and customers are invited to share the map, things improve incalculably as a new map evolves.

I have a good friend who works as a systems architect in a large company. His opinion is that no one should be allowed to design unless they are currently coding. Despite being a senior architect he codes at least one day a week in order to remind himself of the physical implementation. His designs are beautiful to behold.

Customers and developers have respect for him. He is aware of many contexts simultaneously. Whenever he is in one context he has the other in his peripheral vision.

Hierarchy as context

If you are a programmer you will find the next couple of pages easy. If you are not a programmer I hope you will find it interesting and illuminating. Think of it as an experiment in changing context. If you do, you will come out of the next section with a useful understanding of the basics, and the pure, unadulterated feel of what programming is all about.

Since most of our world relies on computer programs of one type or another, this is a useful context to have.

For many programmers programming is a trip into the very nature of logic and consciousness. It is a mirror in which to reduce the world to a set of rules and to examine their interactions.

The programmer's brain in deep concentration is akin to the altered state of consciousness also achieved by deep meditation[69]. They commonly experience time dilation and the loss of a sense of self, almost becoming the code while programming. Many developers experience great leaps of logic in this state and see it as a time of great creativity. The inner detective is doing some of his best work.

Science comes from the Latin word to know or knowledge. Human beings are curious. It is mostly what has driven us to stand up and reach for the stars. We only want to go there to find out what's out there. Curiosity, for us, is a virtue.

The basis of science is taxonomy. Taxonomy is the naming and classification of things. It lends itself very well to hierarchical organisation. I will show you how programming is all about managing hierarchies. Hierarchies are

---

69 De Marco and Lister – Peopleware talks about flow which they identify
   as this deep meditative state of concentration.

arrangements of contexts.

There is a convincing argument that what we consider to be coherent thought is simply the ability to arrange things into classifications.

- Fire belongs to the group of things that burn me.
- Carrots belong to the group of things I can eat.
- Crocodiles belong to the group of things that can eat me.
- This person belongs to the group of people I can trust.
- That person belongs to the group of people that I love.
- The other person belongs to the group of people who are trying to sell me stuff I don't want.

So it goes.

Putting things in the wrong group can be disastrous. Putting a poisonous substance in the "safe-to-eat" group or an enemy with ill will in the "friends-to-be-trusted" group can have disastrous if not fatal consequences. Hence a regular review of the categories and what we hold in them is encouraged by nature.

Noam Chomsky and George P Lakoff famously disagree about the relationship between syntax and grammar. Despite this their work points out that the way our minds work is related to the way we use language. They suggest, in different ways, that the spoken language we use determines the way we think.

This is important because language is mostly about classification and hierarchy.

Object Orientation in context

We are going to follow reality into Object Orientation. We will be applying what we learn to management and organisational structure. When we are able to do that we will have used programming as a metaphor. This will be an easy fit, because the purpose of a software system is to be a metaphor.

Developers spend their lives taking things from one context and translating them into another. Their ability to represent reality as mathematics and metaphor is at the heart of what they do and how they do it.

For many developers the code is a living thing in the sense that there is no real state of being finished. The code needs to be understood and tended.

This is what differentiates software systems from almost any other endeavour. This is what causes many misunderstandings. Software is not a commodity. It is too complex. It needs to change context as the world it inhabits changes context. Fantastically, it can do that and good developers are wizards of change.

This is why many have accepted Extreme Programming with open arms over the last decade. Extreme Programming's built-in acceptance of change, as a consequence of the nature of the endeavour, is powerful.

For many developers it has been a type of existential outing. It was a relief to admit the reality of the situation. Code evolves with its host system and Extreme Programming provides a set of tools to cope with that process. Coding has become like jazz again - controlled freedom.

The very instability that many managers see as a problem is software's greatest strength. To understand the nature of the beast is to know how to manage it. Software is a reflection of the intelligence of the people who write it and as a result must be written in a way that allows it to evolve on two axes:

1. Understanding the requirements of the reality the software serves.
2. Understanding the constant changes to the reality the software serves.

What is seen as instability in software is actually the built-in ability of the software to reflect the reality it serves and to change with it.

Well designed and well built software can be an early warning system that the domain[70] is undergoing change. The software system is a snapshot of the domain. When it starts to exhibit signs of stress you know that something is either changing or about to change. This change has highlighted a distortion, deletion or generalisation in the system that needs attention.

Software built for a deterministic system can approach stability. Very little business software is built for a deterministic system.

Investment in business software is unlike any other investment.

- From the point of view of the investor it is mostly invisible and mysterious.
- Even if it is a perfect fit on delivery it starts degrading immediately.
- Properly tended it will track changes to the domain for a time.
- Like a person getting old it starts to lose elasticity no matter how well it is looked after.
- From my experience 3 to 5 years is the maximum lifespan

---

70 Domain in this context means the environment and purpose of the system. It is what is known about it and where it will operate.

without a heart transplant.

- Expecting a piece of software which is ten or fifteen years old to keep performing on minor maintenance is like expecting a centenarian to run a marathon because you have given them plastic surgery.

Whatever business you are in, if you live in the western world you live in a world where software is involved in everything you do. Understanding how this software sets out to model the world is crucial.

Have you heard the saying that life imitates art? Art is a mirror on life. The two become recursive. The same applies to software in our time. Software was supposed to model business and now business models software. Ring any call centre or communicate with any business and you will find that what can and can't be done is limited by the system.

We are in that translator loop and the prize will go to whoever figures out how to enter the loop and influence the outcome.

We are going on a tour of how software models reality so that we can enter the loop. Object orientation was a major breakthrough. It changed thinking in software design. So, that is what we will explore.

Classes

Things that are gathered together because the attributes they share allow us, in some way, at some level, in some context, to classify them as the same thing. These are called classes. For our purposes let's have a class of all warm blooded living things. Let's call the class "mammals".

Attributes

The things that we know about a mammal that make it

specifically a mammal, or that are worth recording, are called its attributes. For example, the number of legs, habitat, gestation period, sex, and average lifespan.

Methods

The things that a mammal does are called its methods. Moves, eats, reproduces, fights and digests.

Classes of classes

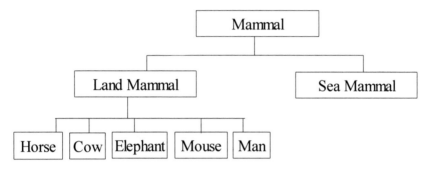

We can decide that we want further classifications into land mammals and sea mammals. We hold the attributes and methods that are common to both, and only those that are common to both, in the Mammals class. What is unique about each classification is held separately in the Land Mammal or the Sea Mammal class.

We can refine both of these classifications into further classes. The same rules, about what goes where, apply. Horses, cows, elephants, mice and men, to name a few. We find enough differences in these types to make them worthy of classifications of their own.

My kingdom for a horse

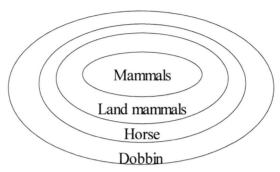

The thing about classes is that they are all onions. They are like Russian dolls. They are hierarchical.

Take Dobbin. He is an object of the horse class. In his horse layer we have his mane colour and whatever is unique to horses as opposed to other land mammals.

Under this layer he has his land mammal layer which holds the information about what is unique to land mammals as opposed to other mammals; but not specific enough to be horsey details.

Under that layer he has a mammal layer which holds information common to all mammals and not specific to land mammals.

Evolution of a class

Now if we discover mammals that lay eggs, we have a couple of choices. Inside the mammal layer we are saying that all mammals have the same birth method. This is no longer true for all mammals.

Context

Our choices are:

1. We can decide to make a new class for egg laying mammals all alone at the same level as mammal. But there are so many other methods and attributes in common that this would seem very wasteful.

2. We can push this method out to the layer of the onion that seems most suitable. Because we have to push it for one, we have to push it for all. We hold place for the birth method but we leave it to the individual sub classes as to how to implement it.

So we push the birth method out to land mammals because the little chap we found is the echidna. It is a little hedgehog-like creature from New Zealand. It lays eggs and happens to be a land mammal.

We face the same problem at the land mammal layer. Egg laying land mammals are as rare as egg laying mammals. We find we want to push the birth method out to the next level of the onion which is the individual layer, the echidna. This means that the birth laying method gets pushed out to horses, cows, elephants, mice and men.

If we were to find out that some behaviour we used to think was different for all mammals was in fact the same we would do the reverse. The "feed young" method for instance might have been held as a local method because we thought all mammals fed their young differently. Now we know they all feed milk to their young, so the method is promoted to the common mammal layer.

There is something going on here called inheritance. Horses, echidnas and elephants all inherit the same behaviour from a common ancestor. They do not have to come up with some behaviours on their own.

Applications

In Object Orientated programming it is exactly the same for a very good reason.

The process necessary to write a system is:

- The domain of the program is analysed and decisions are made about what data and methods should live together.
- Each decision leads to the creation of a class of things.
- The things that all members of the class have in common are promoted to the top of the hierarchy, the centre of the onion.
- When we make an individual it is known as an object, just as Dobbin was an individual example of the class horse.
- As we write the system, evolution starts to take place.
  - → We find we need more and more specialised versions of the class.
  - → We find older versions become obsolete.
  - → We hold on to traits and characteristics.
  - → Some traits proliferate and get promoted up the hierarchy so they can be shared.
  - → Some traits become required only by specialised classes so they get demoted down the hierarchy to where they are specifically needed.
- Inheritance leads to diversity.

We do something called refactoring when we find we need to carry out one of these evolutionary tasks. Two or more classes can merge and become one. One class can be split into two or more. This happens to the traits in a similar way. Methods or abilities can be merged or split. Data structures can merge or be split.

Examining the metaphor

Everything is a metaphor. Sometimes examining the metaphor it tells us more about the thing itself.

Programming creates a metaphor for reality. It is a metaphor that is constantly refining itself. It is a metaphor that remains obviously a metaphor. By examining this metaphor we can examine the art of refinement and apply the metaphor to management.

The secrets of programming

Programming has three main logical constructs.

* Sequence
* Branch
* Loop

Things happen in sequence. There are decision points where the logic branches. There are loops where code repeats until a condition has been satisfied.

No matter how complex code may appear or what paradigm it uses, it will still be made up of sequence, branch and loop. There are ideas of multi-threaded logic where sub-processes are spawned and things happen in parallel. Even then the principles of sequence, branching and looping apply. Threads and parallel processes have to converge and coordinate at certain points before other sequences begin.

Objects in Object Orientated and Aspect Orientated programming which appear to have independent lives are defined by these constructs both at the next level up in the code that gives them context, and in their own internal logic.

Context

Flowcharting a process uses the same three constructs.

There is sequence. Things start and follow a cause and effect existence:

Do X then do Y

There is branching. These are decision points at which either one path or another is followed. Either choice X or Y based on some condition:

If <condition>: do X: else do Y

There is looping. These are repetitions of a process or sequence of processes until a condition is met.

Keep doing X while <condition>: then do Y

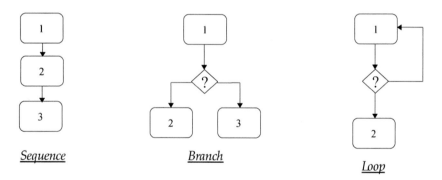

Sequence   *Branch*

Loop

There may be variations on these but when you examine logic it is always some combination of sequence, branching and loop.

If you stop and think about it, all the wizardry of modern technology is built on two solid and easy to understand principles.

Context

1. There is a difference between 1 and 0
2. These three logical constructs

Look around at what we can do with these humble tools: everything from DVD's and digital photography to communication satellites and robotic chess masters. Then consider that we have not even begun to exhaust their potential. So simple, so powerful.

The evolution of programming

Through the years of programming, programmers have discovered a few things about these constructs.

In most programming languages, branches look something like this:

If (condition)	*If it is sunny*
Do (something)	*Have a picnic*
Else	*Else*
Do (something else)	*Eat at home*

We discovered that if we nested too many of these we started to have problems.

```
If(If(If(If(If()))))
or
if(condition){
        Do 1
        if(condition){
                Do 2
                if(condition){
                        if(condition){
                        do "A"
                        }else do "B"
                }else do "C"
        }else do "D"
}else do "E"
```

This is called nesting. Conditions are nested in each other[71].

This complex nesting is akin to taking a one way trip down the trousers of reality. We can become very confused about where we are and start taking decisions at the wrong level.

---

71 Like onions and Russian dolls!

Context

It becomes difficult to understand the logic and very easy to make monumental errors just by leaving out a bracket or putting one in the wrong place. The above example is pretty straightforward in comparison to some of the twists and turns that feral **if's, else's** and **then's** can start producing.

At a high point in the evolution of software development we started to judge code, not by how complex it was, but by how straightforward it is. We stopped counting lines of code as a measure of productivity or functionality and started measuring clarity of intent, suitability for purpose and ease of maintainability.

Professional coders these days measure their code with automated tools to make sure the nesting level does not go too deep. They have statistics that tell them the level of complexity of their code. They spend time and effort keeping the complexity as low as possible and the intent of the code as clear as possible.

Loops look like this:

While(condition)   *While there are oranges*
Do (something)   *Eat another orange*

It can also be expressed as

Do (something)   *Eat another orange*
Until (condition)   *Until no more oranges*

We discovered that although the latter works in many cases, it is not the best code when there are no oranges in the first place.

We can do things in the ***eat another orange*** routine to make sure that it checks for oranges every time at its level of logic. This is extra code and extra processing.

Checking for oranges at the outer loop before we try to eat them results in simpler code, less room for error, quicker execution and better maintainability.

We make sure we go down the correct leg of the trousers of reality in the first instance.

Early programs were full of what were termed *go-to* constructs. These seemed like a good idea at the time. Very early programming was about physically wiring bits of machine together. This progressed to examining the contents of physical memory which involved mostly *going-to* those bits of memory and manipulating them with machine friendly language.

As software development evolved this became wrapped in more human friendly language. We progressed up the hierarchy. We bundled often repeated things together in the verbs of the computer language and developed a grammar.

Go-to was a hangover from a different world and was still possible in the macro level languages we had, by then, achieved.

Unfortunately, jumping all over a program and ignoring sequence, made the medium too complex and thus limited the complexity of the logic possible[72]. Errors became far too difficult to track and fix as the contortions of the code were undisciplined and erratic.

Go to was consigned to history by the common consent of

---

72 I talked specifically about this in the chapter on Balance. One side goes up the other comes down. If the medium is complex and the use is complex, you get complexity squared.

coders themselves. Control was exercised and freedom ensued.

Once sequence was established and the languages were simplified, what could be done with them started to grow exponentially.

At each stage of evolution the previous level was refined and encapsulated into a much simpler interface.

This process continues. At one time a programmer could spend days changing the value of a memory register. Now one word in one statement can change the contents of thousands of memory registers.

Hierarchy in programming is not a measurement of importance but a measure of encapsulation. Programmers have learned that you can only encapsulate what you have refined. Errors will be magnified by levels of hierarchy sitting on top of it. It is important to get the basics right.

Because of this refinement, a single programmer can do in a few seconds what it once would have taken a team of programmers weeks to do. If this programmer has been working in the business for more than a few years he or she can remember working in those teams.

As the power of what can be done increases with the refinement and encapsulation of logic tools, the expectations grow. It still takes teams of programmers to deliver the systems that are required of them. These programmers and tools deliver increasingly sophisticated functionality in an increasingly demanding marketplace.

No matter how complex these systems get, no matter how many layers of tools there are between the developer and the machine code, the same rules of logic are still in play. The machine looks at differences between 1 and 0 and the developer creates sequence, branches and loops that are metaphors for the real world logic that the computer is serving.

Hierarchy is an onion (part 2)

The centre of the onion is the top of the hierarchy. The top of the hierarchy holds the centre together. This is essential in software and in life.

> *"Things fall apart; the centre cannot hold;*
> *Mere anarchy is loosed upon the world,"*
> The Second Coming
> William Butler Yeats

The organisation in context

Because of the way we perceive hierarchies we tend to see the top as the most important. Think of an organisational hierarchy. Is there a presupposition that the tip top has been filtered from the rest?

We think in terms of competition so we see the winner at the top. We tend to see this person as the most skilled person: THE BOSS. We believe that people have to rise through the hierarchy and be better at everything than everybody else.

Why do they have to rise through the hierarchy? Why do people who are more specialised have to become more generalised? Certainly people who are able to see the big picture from this perspective are invaluable. It is a specialisation of its own. I am going to propose a different type of organisational representation.

Management and evolution

Evolution moves toward adaptation and specialisation through trial and error. What succeeds survives. This is called natural selection.

If we represent the company organisation as an object model hierarchy, then a manager should only have those attributes that are common to all employees of the company. A manager should not have attributes or methods that belong elsewhere in the hierarchy. Each employee should be able to peel back layers and reveal an inner manager.

Metaphors are just metaphors. Programming is a metaphor for "how things work in the world" so that we can explore the idea of the inner onion of management.

Now consider abstraction and inheritance in Management.

Abstraction

The dictionary definition of abstract is this:

Expressing a quality or characteristic apart from any specific object or instance.

An abstract class in programming is something of which we can say: it contains only things it has in common with all the classes that are inherited from it.
These include the attributes and methods that the base class holds to be true about all members of this class, regardless of their specialisation.

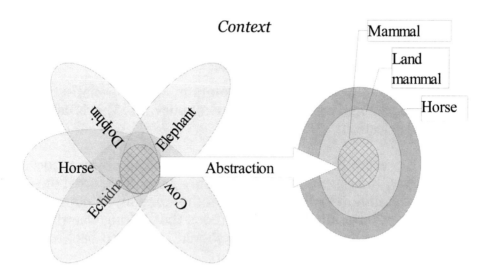

Context

Mammal

Land mammal

Horse

Dolphin

Elephant

Horse

Echidna

Cow

Abstraction

Abstraction

We can create abstraction at every level. We can create an abstraction of land mammal. We can have an abstraction of horse that is all those things common to all horses. The abstraction will hold abstractions of all the previous layers. The central abstraction must be true of all the following layers.

The abstraction is a very refined version of the class.

You can begin to see how important it is that we get this right. Programming is a constant maintenance job. If we construct our classes with professional diligence and refinement, we can promote and demote attributes and abilities as evolution indicates. It requires uncluttered thinking, uncluttered code and uncluttered management.

It is a case of constant refinement. In the example, the echidna has broadened our understanding of mammals. It lays eggs and is still a mammal. There is no standard birth method that holds true for all mammals. Therefore the birth method has to move from the central mammal abstract layer.

222

It really belongs in the more specialised layer.

In another sort of refinement we decide that the "feed young" method is not so specialised and can be moved from specialisation into the general mammal layer.

In this way we are constantly striving for balance between the big picture and the detail, and where things belong, as our understanding of a domain evolves.

Refactoring is a powerful tool in all this. It allows us to stabilise the centre and maintain the critical interfaces. Interfaces are lines of communication.

The great big advantage of code is that it is mutable. It can be changed, and should be designed to change as understanding and evolution require it to.

This is also the great big advantage of being human.

Virtual and pure virtual

The dictionary definition of virtual is:
Being such in essence or effect though not formally recognized or admitted

A virtual method is one that can be overridden by the inherited class. So in the onion of horse there is a run method.

If all land mammals run, then the land mammal layer will know that there is a basic running method which involves moving legs in a coordinated way.

At the horse level of the onion this may not be enough. It may need specific information about the horse's number of legs and direction of the knee joint and a number of other local attributes. The generic run method can be overwritten at this horse layer.

In this context we mean something that is a working place-holder for the real thing which could come along at any moment.

It is used when you know that everything derived from this point on must have certain characteristics, even though you are not sure what they are. You know enough to make a guess that will function; but you let specialists, who will have more relevant knowledge, come up with their own method. You know that a horse will have to run. Horses are experts at horse running. So you leave the details up to the horse.

Think of it as a baby foal knowing that running is standing up and moving legs. Picture a baby horse trying to run with tangled legs and furious intent. As it grows it rewrites the method until it achieves the flowing grace that almost all humans admire in the marriage of muscle and movement that is a horse at full speed.

A pure virtual method is one that you know all your descendants must have. You know that they will all do it so differently that you have no way of even giving them a working place holder.

Take the "move" method at the mammal layer. You want all of them to move. You do not want it to be a local decision as to whether to move or not. You declare a pure virtual function that makes it obligatory that the specialists find a way to do it. If not you will not allow them to exist.

In our horse example we could also consider a dolphin. We know if our mammals can't move they will either starve or be eaten.

Standing still and waiting for food to come to you, or waiting around to be made into a coffee table, is fine for plants but not for mammals.

We don't even suggest which limbs to move because dolphins and whales move very well indeed without legs. Horses, on the other limb, can wave their tails all day but they are unlikely to achieve noticeable velocity that way.

Scope and privacy

Privacy. Every class has a right to private methods and attributes. These are things about the class that are inviolate. They are things that you can not tell the class to do nor ask it to disclose to you. They are things that are used by the internal logic of the class's methods.

For example, with Dobbin we can not ask him to digest his food nor ask him to tell us why he won't drink even if we have led him to water.

These are private matters to him. To get at them we would have to open him up and that would destroy him. We can ask him to run the "eat" function or the "drink" function. He will know whether he is hungry or thirsty and his autonomic system will call the "digest" function as part of the public "eat" function. It comes from somewhere in his evolution. He inherited digest from mammal.

The point is that the parent class can have private functions and may or may not be an abstract class. You could have an instance of a generic mammal that has private functions that work in a way they do not work for classes that inherit from it. When you instantiate it there may be things it has to do in order to have an independent existence and have a useful function.

Put another cap on the metaphor

✔ We can gather things into classes of things by putting like with like.

✔ Classes can parent other classes which are more specialised versions of themselves and which have more functionality.

✔ The children have the attributes and abilities of their parents[73] as well as their own attributes and abilities.

✔ We can change where in the hierarchy we define methods. Children can have more specialised versions of parent methods.

✔ Parent classes can give a general outline and then trust their child classes to do things that they themselves do not know how to do.

✔ This classification is an ongoing and self perfecting process

We can take the metaphor to the next step and do a round trip by taking the rules of Object Orientated programming and applying them to management. We will do this in a moment so that we will have a clearer idea of what management might be all about.

We want to know what management and organisation might be if we take them at their purest form, like triple distilled whiskey without the impurities of ego, megalomania, fear, paranoia, pessimism and cynicism. Once these are gone we will add generosity, confidence, trust, optimism and hope as our impurities of choice.

---

73 Of course you can have multiple inheritance but experienced programmers find clever ways around this because the relationships are too hard to manage if they go wrong – for instance when both parents have the same method – which one does the child take? As in nature developers have found clever ways to determine the dominant genes.

226

Theory X and theory Y[74].

Theory X: People are basically lazy and need to be bullied into working.

Theory Y: People enjoy work and will try to be creative and forward thinking.

Both of these tend to be a self-fulfilling prophesy. People largely react to the way you treat them. People tend to justify the trust given to them.

Henry Ford said "Whether you think you can or that you can't, you are usually right". It could be extended to "Whether you think your team can or that they can't, you are almost always right".

Bill Strickland's[75] story is amazing. He is a truly inspiring person. His life's work is to inspire. He set out to do something for disadvantaged people in Pittsburgh. In the course of this he proved something quite astonishing:

Regardless of people's education or background, if you put them in a world class environment with flowers, good food, sunshine, art, music, beautiful furniture and opportunity, you get world class behaviour. It is worthwhile following the link provided and listening to Mr Strickland telling the story himself.

Hierarchy, context and organisation charts

Think of the organisation chart where you work if there is one. If there is it probably looks something like the following:

---

74 *The Human Side of Enterprise* by Douglas McGregor
75 http://www.manchesterguild.org/indexflash.htm

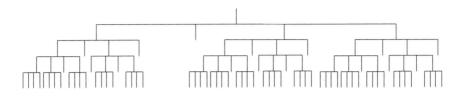

You probably have the big boss at the top and a proliferation of branches beneath him. Responsibility appears to flow downwards[76] and authority upwards.

Even if your organisation has authority flowing downwards and responsibility flowing upwards, I bet that most people see themselves on an upward trajectory. Those that don't at least "pretend to" are considered to have no ambition and to have reached a career dead end.

There are several curious assumptions in this model of organisations.

The first is that there is literally an up and down to this thing.

The second is that the lower you are, the less worth you have, and that you must strive to move up.

The third is that the people at the top are more specialised than the people at the bottom.

If we were to regard this organisation diagram as a class hierarchy diagram, how would that change our perception of it? In a class hierarchy diagram, as we have seen, classes inherit methods and attributes from classes earlier in the hierarchy and then they specialise and evolve.

---

76 i.e. Management exercises command and control and then pushes the buck down – which is to put the blame on those with least control over direction and outcome. Good managers hold on to the buck and give their people room to succeed.

Context

It may seem preposterous to suggest that technicians are more evolved than Chief Executive Officers, unless you understand that evolution is about diversity, refinement and specialisation.

Hello, can you hear me?

Flat structures do not really work either. The lines of communication get too long and function becomes confused. If they all try to use a single point of contact it fuses pretty quickly, especially if it is a person.

Chinese whispers are worse. People start to form local hierarchies based on function no matter what it says on the chart.

Whatever you are told, specialisation is necessary and a node network of communication is necessary to filter information by function in both directions.

Imagine if the hierarchy, currently a hierarchy of people, were to be a hierarchy of capabilities. Wherever you are in your company's hierarchy, imagine a company hierarchy which represented the classification of skills.

There are two things I ask you to remember:

✔ Anyone who is a functioning human being and does not live alone on a mountain top has management skills
✔ Anyone who is a functioning human being and does not live alone on a mountain top has interpersonal skills

229

Context

Imagine if everyone in your organisation had a base set of skills that grew rather than shrank as they specialised.

I would put management and communication skills as the base abstract class. Finance and business acumen would be in there. Specialisation would only occur as function demanded.

Now put the people back on the tree and you will discover something interesting. The further down the tree you go the bigger the onion you become. You may have less responsibility but you will have more methods at your disposal.

Imagine how it would be to turn this around. Currently it appears that people who manage worry about how much they know or don't know about the specialisations of those they are managing. Imagine if the people being managed understood management and communications as part of their core skills.

It would be easier to manage people by consent. It would be easier to find those with a real skill in management. Management would be recognised as the service it is.

Look at some of the potential benefits of having everyone in the company trained in a set of common capabilities

- ✔ Estimation
- ✔ Communication
- ✔ Planning
- ✔ Prioritisation
- ✔ Decision making
- ✔ Lateral thinking
- ✔ Business acumen
- ✔ Budget management
- ✔ Assertiveness
- ✔ Time management
- ✔ Interpersonal skills
- ✔ Vertical and horizontal thinking

Ask anyone involved in business coaching and you will find that the main problems organisations face today are not of technical skill or cognitive ability but of communication.

Among the benefits of a common set of capabilities would be

- ✔ Easier and more effective communication.
- ✔ People have management skills to be promoted if they are ready and if they want to move to management.
- ✔ Level playing field for promotions and easier to determine individual ability based on capabilities.
- ✔ Separate wheat from chaff so that only high quality, relevant information is being communicated along communication lines.
- ✔ Managers who make decisions will have processed data to work with.
- ✔ Little time wasted on trivia.
- ✔ Decisions made at appropriate level by responsible individuals.
- ✔ Coaching and peer review become the norm enabling local processing and quality control.

✔ Rapid communication.
✔ Filtering of content of ideas.
✔ Ease the decision making process.
✔ Managers managing by exception.
✔ Job boundaries are filters not demarcation lines.
✔ Focus on common outcome.
✔ Effective and appropriate delegation in both directions.
✔ Effective and appropriate retention of responsibility in both directions.
✔ Reduction of waste.
✔ Improved moral.
✔ Improved productivity.

There would be a balancing flow in the other direction. Some of the abstract skills required to manage are also technical[77] things like

✔ The rules of good design
✔ The rules of sequence, iteration and branching
✔ Shared metaphors
✔ Working knowledge of current technology

It is essential that we consider:

• How to achieve this
• The role of competition
• The truth about control
• Methodology myths
• Feedback
• The nature of evolution

---

77 There is a need to be technically competent because of the growing dependence of business on computer systems

A modest proposal

Take your organisational chart and turn it upside down.

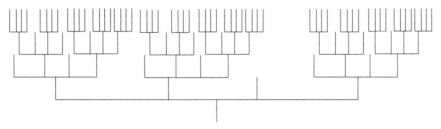

- Management capabilities are pure virtual: universally required.
- Management capabilities are abstract: communicable and responsive to change.
- Management capabilities are refined with experience.
- Management capabilities are inherited by the entire organisation.

The manager is the root not the apex. The manager is the abstract class that leads by inspiration and functions by being the balance point.

Really think about the implications of this. Think about the implications for power. If you understand the nature or power you will know that confidence and restraint are the ultimate expressions of power.

"Power is like being a lady... if you have to tell people you are, you aren't."
Margaret Thatcher

Power is when you have every justification to kill someone, and then you don't."
Oskar Shindler

Neural Pathways

We have a hundred billion[78] neurons in our brain.

100,000,000,000.

When we have any experience we make new connections between some of these neurons.

When we think the same way or behave the same way repeatedly, we strengthen these neural pathways. The more you do something, the easier it is to continue doing it. The law of balance tells us that if this gets easier, alternatives get harder to contemplate.

Have you ever experienced this? Do you do something that way because that is the way you do it?

A hundred billion is a lot of choice. A hundred billion is a lot of potential.

Remember that control is flexibility of approach. Control is to have a choice about what you do and what way you do it. Control is freedom of choice. Control is freed will. Control is freedom. Controlled freedom is the destination of great artists, great scientists, great leaders, great thinkers and a great part of the rest of us.

---

78 An American billion is 10^9. A European billion 10^{12}. Now depending on how you want to play this you could argue that Europeans have more brain cells because the statement is that we have 100 billion brain cells and in America that is 100,000,000,000 while in Europe one hundred billion is 100,000,000,000,000. A difference of 99,900,000,000,000. I imagine my American friends might want to assert that Americans have more brain cells because self admittedly Europeans have 100 thousand million, while Americans have gone for the sensible option of having 100 billion. Either way the deep structure and the number of brain cells is 10^{11}.

Hierarchy of decisions

We make decisions all the time. Even doing nothing is a decision. Every decision has a set of consequences. When you make a decision you create a pathway through potential connections. Variety of behaviour gives you a variety of connections. This variety gives you control. Variety comes from creativity. Creativity gives you control.

Plans

"Prediction is very difficult, especially about the future" – Niels Bohr

Nothing happens in a vacuum. Nothing happens without consequence. Everything has a consequence.

There are some interesting arguments about the nature of reality. Is it deterministic or not? If it is deterministic, meaning everything happens as a result of the inevitable physics of particles set in motion by the big bang, then we have no free will.

It is hard to accept this. It would imply no morality, no accountability and no choice. Are our brains really just rationalisation machines that sit in our head observing and telling us "I meant to do that!"?

There is mounting evidence that this is not the case. It is easy to misunderstand quantum physics but it does imply that the universe is not deterministic. Certainly not the universe we observe anyway. We apparently do have the ability to affect the outcome. It may take more will than we previously thought though.

Context

We have amazing abilities to make predictions. We create a model of how we think the future will turn out and we play with the prediction. We can mentally change variables, reactions and probabilities.

A plan is a map of the future. It is a map of an undiscovered country. It is a map of one possible pathway through the future. A neural pathway.

This map is made up of a number of decisions you propose and project. You guess at the outcomes of these decisions based on experience and calculation.

The decisions you predict are predicted in a hierarchy. X will lead to Y which will mean we will have to decide on Z and that will present an opportunity of P then Q which will mean we can have J, A and M tomorrow.

The consequences are exponential. As the plan goes away into the future, the probability diminishes of everything happening just as you predict. This is because you have two problems:

- The proliferation of things you have to predict.
- The increasing rate of change as you advance into the future.

In your plan, each branch or loop in the logic is a nexus. A nexus is a point of changing probability. At that nexus there are a set of possible outcomes of that decision and a set of probable outcomes.

You may have a final outcome in mind when you get to a nexus, but the outcomes at any level in the hierarchy can throw new light on that final outcome. It is prudent to reassess and reevaluate regularly.

We need to consider that there are interim outcomes and final outcomes. In its own right each interim outcome is a final outcome. In the continuing now of reality each final outcome is really only an interim outcome to the next level. Nothing exists in isolation.

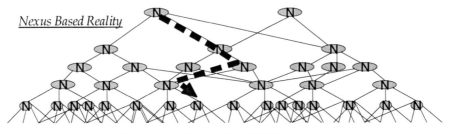

Nexus Based Reality

Nexus Based Decision Making

If these new outcomes at this nexus do not now show a way to the original planned outcome you still have some choices.

- You can stick to your plan regardless. An interesting test is to ask yourself: If you were to start the plan from here, would you take the path the plan currently indicates? If the answer is that you would not; and if you do choose to stick to your guns; one or more of the following must be true:
  - → There are enough of the original outcomes reachable and you can change the scope of the plan.
  - → You are prepared to settle for the new set of outcomes.
  - → You believe that hoping for the best is sufficient action.
  - → You like being a hostage to fortune.
  - → You are going claim success prematurely, leave the project and let someone else take the rap.
  - → You do not want the project to succeed.
- You can insist on the outcome you want even though it is not reachable from here. You will pay much more than you had anticipated because you have to try to change reality to

get it. Eventually you will arrive back at choice number 1 again.

- You can step back up the hierarchy to the point at which you can see a path to your desired set of outcomes. If you are a master planner this will only be one step back at most because you check in with reality regularly
  - → You use short feedback loops as a way of checking your compass regularly and making corrections at the earliest possible nexus.
  - → You may not be able to have all of your outcomes from any nexus at the next level. You may need to split your plan into a number of trips from a crucial nexus. This is a strategy of making frequent deliveries containing prioritized outcomes until you have enough outcomes to satisfy the original need.
  - → You may not be able to see the end-game from this nexus, just the next set of nexus. Then you can adopt a strategy of carrying on down the hierarchy with limited expectations and little baggage and coming back with a detailed map of that route. There are some tools that you can use to do this. (See list below).
  - → You realize that others may have knowledge and maps of upcoming nexus so you see planning as a collaborative game.

Tools for exploring the hierarchy:

- ✔ Tracer bullets
  - ☑ Coined as a technique in "The Pragmatic Programmer" by Andrew Hunt and David Thomas.
  - ☑ In artillery you either calculate everything up front before you fire and hope you got it right and you will hit the target; or you can use tracer bullets which are phosphorous rounds which light up and show you where your bullets are landing so that you can adjust your aim

before you commit everything. They can also be used by platoon leaders to demonstrate where firepower should be concentrated.

☑In Software development you can deliver a lightweight end to end solution. This normally consists of skeleton code with basic functionality which gives your customer some idea what the finished product will be like. This can be adjusted at low cost until your customer is satisfied. Then all of the expensive functionality can be added.

Don't fire bullets – build bridges!
I prefer to be less militaristic in my metaphors for customers, so I use the term guide-wire when explaining this concept to them.

The bridge over Royal Gorge in Colorado is the highest suspension bridge in the world at 321 meters. It was built in 1929. There is a thousand tonnes of steel in the floor of the bridge.

I visited it in 1998 and as I gazed into the gorge from the bridge I wondered how on earth they did it. I found an information post that told me.

They got one cable across the gorge. They used this to get things back and forth. They built the bridge around it; and that original guide-cable is still in the bridge.

✔ Spike solutions

☑ Coined by Kent Beck author of "*Extreme Programming Explained: Embrace Change*"

☑ This is a small focussed effort to explore a possibility or to solve a problem.

☑ The effort spikes.

☑ It is usual to allow people to step outside of the current project constraints to do something which will provide clarity.

☑ Alistair Cockburn calls this "Clear the fog".

✔ Very light prototyping

☑ Very similar to spike solutions.

☑ Prototyping assumes you are building a first attempt to prove the theory. It assumes you will throw it away when the real one gets underway. It is better to build something you can refactor and reuse.

☑ If you are prototyping to throw away, make sure you make it out of the equivalent of balsa wood and that you control the amount of time spent on the prototype.

✔ Pilots

☑ Pick a small uncomplicated implementation to test the waters, as it were.

✔ Short feedback loops

☑ Short iterations of achievable goals.

☑ Test first approach – In software development you write the tests before you write the code. This can be applied to almost everything. I have applied it to carpentry, writing fiction, gardening, singing, training, coaching and many other things.

✔ Frequent small deliveries

☑ Organise yourself and whatever you are doing so that you can deliver parts of it independently and often. This has the advantage that your customer sees progress and that you get ongoing gratification and feedback.

✔ Collaboration
☑ In the sense of exploring possible routes, collaboration is a great friend. If you are hiding what you are doing and competing with others you will not get proper feedback. Collaborate freely with:
  ☛ Customers.
  ☛ You own team members.
  ☛ Other teams.
  ☛ Stakeholders.
  ☛ Anyone who is able and willing to give high quality feedback.
  ☛ Peers.
  ☛ Managers.
  ☛ Coaches.
  ☛ Consultants.
  ☛ Domain experts.
✔ PERT and CPA.
  ☑ Project Evaluation and Review Technique and Critical Path Analysis.
  ☑ Developed in the 1950's by the US Navy to manage complex projects.
  ☑ PERT looks at tasks in terms of
    ☛ Optimistic time
    ☛ Pessimistic time
    ☛ Most likely time
    ☛ Slack
  ☑ CPA looks at the time it will take to do those tasks that have finish-start dependencies between them. It seeks to find the shortest possible path to completion.
  ☑ WARNING: This tool is a hangover from Scientific Management. It can lead to Gantt charts and "big design up front". I include it because if used in the spirit of the other tools mentioned here it can be a powerful ally.

☑ Use it to explore relationships between tasks and to identify any necessary sequence.

☑ Remember

- ☛ The time estimates are highly subjective.
- ☛ Like all plans it is a better map of where you have been than where you are going.
- ☛ You will probably end up doing a different set of things than those you put on your first or many subsequent PERT charts.
- ☛ Use it in small iterations and then only to clarify. Keep the detail scarce. Use it to spot the equivalent of cities, motorways and large geographical features on your map of your project or endeavour.
- ☛ PERT and CPA are a boon if you have unmoveable milestones or if you need to plan for expensive or difficult to acquire resources like a crane or a plumber.

The most useful strategy is to use lateral thinking. You can jump across to another nexus and have a look at the potential routes from another perspective.

This type of strategy gives you the option to appear to move across rather than reversing. In reality you tend to have to back up in order to move across even if it is only metaphorically.

There is a section on lateral thinking in the earlier chapter entitled "The Key".

Plans represent only one potential route through an almost infinite combination of possibilities. What happens when reality catches up and your projection proves to have been inaccurate? After all even the best laid plans of mice and men often go awry[79].

---

79 Adapted from the Robert Burns poem - "To a Mouse" - "The best laid

If you are forcing your outcomes and pretending to be somewhere else, consequences will start to accumulate. To try to keep going along the predicted pathway under these circumstances is not only stubborn it is foolhardy.

If you have lost sight of the desired outcome but some of the small outcomes appear to be right ones, this is because reality is not always a one to one relationship between cause and

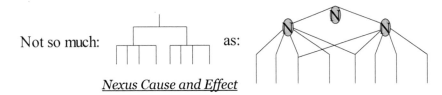

Not so much: ... as:

Nexus Cause and Effect

What you reach from this position may also be reachable from another position. Bear in mind that the meta point I am making here is that there are many potential paths to your outcome so it is not surprising that there are different nexus which lead to the same outcomes or partial outcomes.

If you are not where you expected to be, you may be able to put corrections and new layers into the hierarchy of your plan. These might enable it to work out after all.

It is also worth bearing in mind that you probably do not need all the outcomes at each layer. You may have the opportunity to branch to a nexus that dispenses with the unwanted outcomes.

---

schemes o' mice an' men/ gang aft a-gley"

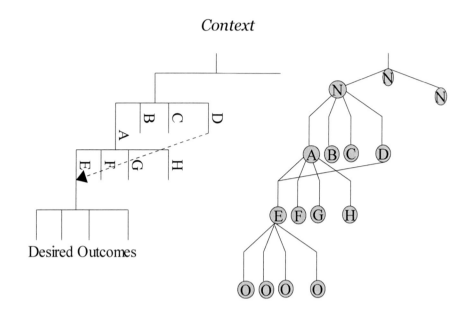

Desired Outcomes

A has outcomes E, F, G and H
D only has outcome E
If you only require E, then F, G and H are overheads.
You might well consider D rather than the planned A

<u>*Nexus Branches*</u>

By the same reasoning your plan can loop causing confusion between cause and effect. TOC tools are extremely handy here for weeding out unwanted symptoms[80].

---

80 "Evaporating cloud" and "Root cause analysis" in particular.

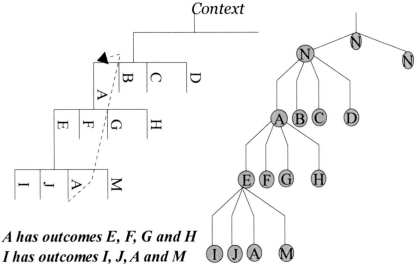

A has outcomes E, F, G and H
I has outcomes I, J, A and M

If you are iterating your plans, this is not necessarily a problem.
It is an indication of confusion if it continues without progress.
You may want to do some root cause analysis to find out what
mistaken assumptions you could have been making about the
decisions in A.
You may want to explore B, C or D as being more direct routes to
your outcomes.
You may want to move back to the nexus before A and take an
entirely different route.
Loops are good because they help you identify where change is
necessary.

Nexus Loops

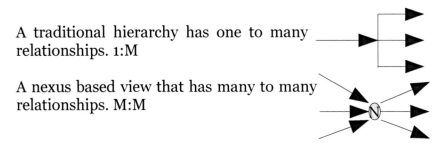

A traditional hierarchy has one to many
relationships. 1:M

A nexus based view that has many to many
relationships. M:M

Nexus Based Relationships

245

This means that a nexus can connect to anything. Branches in a traditional hierarchy just branch. In reality there are many ways to skin a cat and you need a plan that reflects this.

A single step, sequential, unidirectional branch view is a waterfall. The only way to negotiate it is out of control in a barrel. In reality, plans often need to do things which require iterative, parallel and multi-directional thinking - a manoeuvrable kayak and a good set of paddles.

Plans should be evolving as they uncover truth and this is achieved by some of the iteration practices of Agile

You should be constantly reassessing priorities of particular tasks by focussing on the outcomes rather than the tasks.

People who use a plan as a script rather than a map can get very lost. When you were use the plan as a map you can use it to see that the territory is changing.

It is best if you do not invest in an expensive detailed map. You want a map that only shows you landmarks that are unlikely to change. You need one with lots of space so that you can fill in the details as they become visible in front of you.

When things go wrong go back to the last nexus. This will be just before things started to go wrong. It is best if you do not have to step back too far. This makes it a good idea to check your position and progress as often as possible.

In Agile, particularly Extreme Programming, developers use short iterations, constant testing, constant integration, test first and collaboration to achieve just this.

The bad news is that Reality can be more flexible than your

plan. The good news is that Reality can be more flexible than your plan.

The plan is only a map and, more than that, it is a map that needs updating. Since there are so many variables at play here in predicting the future, the emphasis is better placed on knowing where you are.

To quote Granny Weatherwax[81], you can not be lost if you know where you are; even if everywhere else gets lost on you.

If you know where you are, you can always work out how you got there and how to get to where you want to go from there. Reality is awash with potential. Why limit yourself to one unchangeable course of action? Why gamble your future on guesses when you can know some things?

- Know where you are.
- Know where you started from.
- Know where you want to get to.
- Know how to test if you are still en route.
- Know where you are in relation to where you started
- Know where you are in relation to where you want to get to.
- Know how to plot a new course.
- Know when to plot a new course.
- Know how to take advantage of opportunities.
- Know how to traverse hyper space when a wormhole[82] opens up
- Know what that trip in hyper space means in real space

---

81 Another of Terry Pratchett's amazing Discworld personae. Granny is a witch who represents common sense. Although she is the most powerful witch she prefers "headology" to magic. She has an unshakeable belief in herself.

82 Intuition, creative leaps, inspiration and sitting bolt upright at 4 in the morning with a great idea are all wormholes.

Communication in context

Have you ever found yourself talking at cross purposes to someone else? Were you negotiating some logical tangent when suddenly you found yourself in a full blown disagreement over something unexpected?

Have you ever felt that it was as if, at some stage, the other party had stopped understanding the basic meanings of words?

Have you ever been surprised by somebody's reaction to something that you had thought could not possibly cause offence?

Have you ever found that rather than getting at the heart of the matter, you were arguing strongly for something which was not what you really want to talk about in the first place?

It appears that many people have had this experience. It seems to most affect those areas where you need the cooperation of others. Even discussions between friends and acquaintances can rapidly escalate into quite emotional outpourings.

Many of us want to be able to communicate our point of view to others. We tend to believe we are right and we quite often take a run up to it in order to try to set the stage for our message.

When you are leading people it is imperative that you have some sort of common agreement as to what you are trying to achieve together. If they start disappearing down the rabbit hole of some detail when you need to get things moving, your ability to communicate is going to be put to the test. I have seen teams mutinying on some poor manager who never quite got to the point of what he was trying to tell them.

I have also had the great fortune to work with people and for people who seem to be able to express themselves clearly. This has the effect of clarifying purpose and of getting people working towards one goal. They seem to be able to talk in a language that engages, instructs and directs unambiguously. What are these people doing that is different and how can we achieve the same effect while continuing to be ourselves?

A good start is the art of working in pairs on tasks within teams. A manager often has to play the role of parent or referee between intelligent and competent individuals. Left to themselves some of these people can compromise their own ability to achieve success by continuing to discuss and disagree over trivialities. There are other individuals who pair up and seem to communicate instinctively.

It is a great experience to work with people who just seem to be on the same wavelength and whose project is almost assured of success as it comes out of the starting gate.

It is less than wonderful to work with people who seem to encourage rebellion just by saying good morning. These people need to be managed. If you take the time you will find that they are perfectly nice people who are reviled and resented by reasonable and normally tolerant colleagues. They tend to be either totally unaware of their effect or to be totally mystified by it. It is not as if they set out to create problems or disagreement.

Some people just seem to click. They have an ability to communicate clearly. They can gauge the temperature of the group. They can get their meaning across without losing popularity, regardless of the message. In fact many times rather than shoot the messenger, their colleagues and friends seem to embrace them even more closely the worse the news or the bigger the task they bring.

Why is this? Wouldn't it be useful to be one of the communicators?

Dreams

"In dreams begin responsibility"

W.B.Yeats

I had a dream last night. Have you ever had a dream that follows you all day? Sometimes you can remember it as if it actually happened, can't you? Have you ever had the sort where you have a big row with someone in the dream and you both say unpleasant and hurtful things? Isn't it just a bit awkward when you meet them at the coffee bar later in the day, and they are really nice to you?

There is the other kind of dreams too. Sometimes you know immediately that you never were in ancient Rome or that you don't currently exist as a twelve dimensional shape. There are abstract dreams and dreams of flying where you suddenly remember how to ignore gravity?

When you realise you are in a dream you can change the rules? In the dream once you realise what is going on, you are in control of what happens just by thinking about it.

You think: "It would be great if the thing chasing me turned into a lemon meringue pie". Instantly one bit of the dream gets put on hold. By thinking of Lemon Meringue pie you are in a café with your best friend on free lemon meringue pie day.

When you do remember about the chase and decide to do the decent thing and go back to see how it was resolved, you seem to have a new set of rules. The pie turns out to be a bus conductor and when you show him your ticket he wishes you a good day just before you wake up!

In my dream last night I was walking down the road. In my dream someone stopped their car to give me a lift. I could not see the face. Imagine it was you.

We went to my destination and discovered that you needed a lift home because your car turned into a lemon meringue pie. I gave you a lift on my bike to the point from which you could get home comfortably on foot. As I parked my bike in the garage my father appeared and asked me why I did not take you the whole way home.

In my dream I told him that you did not want me to. You enjoyed the walk when you could get home in time for tea. In my dream I was also you, walking along the sunny road, approaching a crossroads with a wooden signpost.

Our mind is continuously making sense of the world. If you like you can think of your mind as the thing that joins the right and the left hemispheres of your brain.

Right brain is creative and deals in symbols and metaphors. It is subjective. Surprisingly enough it also allows you to see the big picture. This implies that good managers have to access and exercise the right brain.

The left brain is logical and mathematical. It is objective. It deals with words, language and patterns. It allows you to appreciate detail.

There are some theories that suggest that people are either left brain or right brain dominant[83].

We are able to switch between big picture and detail, between objective and subjective, between metaphor and mathematical. We have the ability to view people and situations from multiple perspectives.

Our intelligence, consciousness and creative spark lies in the negotiation of these two sides of the brain.

Gregory Bateson said, in a lecture in 1974, that a dream is a "statement in the language of things". He said that the things mentioned are not the things referred to. The truth in the dream is the relationships contained in it. He was saying that how we represent the connections between things is more important to us than how we represent the things themselves.

Dreams are about connections. Hierarchies are about connections. In the nexus model I proposed above, the neural web of reality is all about connections.

The advantage of focussing on connections is that it frees you from content, attachment and detail. Although you need a certain amount of content you also need to be able to recognise patterns. Looking at patterns is a short cut to appreciating the big picture and being able to change perspective and find a better way.

Perspectives

There are rules we make for ourselves. Sometimes we know about them and sometimes we do not. Some of these rules are

---

83 http://www.intelliscript.net/test_area/questionnaire/questionnaire.c
    gi?q=right_brain_left_brain_2
  and http://www.web-us.com/BRAIN/braindominance.htm

important to us and sometimes they are only functional in context and so they are temporary. Some are based on unconscious prejudice and some are based on thoughtful analysis. Some of them overstay their welcome by hiding in the attic.

Have a look at this Johari Window[84]

	What I know about myself that others know	What I don't know about myself that others know
Public ↑	What I know about myself that others don't know	What don't I know about myself that others don't know

Unconscious →

Johari Window

The things we know about are easier to comprehend and to manage in ourselves and in others. The real challenge is to manage the rules that are not so obvious or logical.

What do you do when people do not capitulate to your ineffable logic? What do you do when they acknowledge your logic and it still does not make a blind bit of difference to them?

Well first of all you have to be able to see the world from their point of view. In order to understand their point of view and behaviour you need to be able to understand that they have rules that are not yours. They also have rules they themselves do not know they have. So do you.

When I talk to groups of people there is almost always

---

84 Developed by Joseph Luft and Harry Ingham as a cognitive psychology tool. Charles Handy also refers to it in his work and is most interested in the bottom right quadrant which is the most mysterious.

someone who feels uncomfortable with "touchy feely stuff". Some people can find it unnecessary and want to go directly to pragmatic details. This happens for a number of reasons.

- Some people want a simple set of rules they can follow. At the same time they are following a set of complex internal rules and relationships.
- If what you are saying or proposing challenges someone's conscious or unconscious rules, they may feel uncomfortable and they will reflexively want to dismiss it.
- People mix up the levels of their rules. For some reason we can unconsciously promote some minor rule to a false level of priority.
- Many people who consider themselves left brained have a right brain ability that they are mistakenly trying to suppress.
- People think they do not like labels or rules but they have unconsciously labelled themselves and their rules are very important to them at some level.
- Some people are also fearful of being hurt because from childhood they have been warned not to wear their heart on their sleeve. The adults, who, consciously or unconsciously, create this rule of repression, are missing the point that managing emotions is managing the big picture. To have controlled freedom in your emotions you must first of all get to know them. People who are familiar with their emotions and emotional responses are more able to manage the negative emotions and reactions in themselves and others.

In my experience the people who react most dismissively or violently to this sort of approach and subject matter, are almost always the people who came back later to ask me for more details. Why might this be do you think?

Training rules to behave

When you are learning how to code you have to work a lot of things through. In order to understand what it is all about you need both theoretical and experiential learning. Just reading code in a book is not enough. You need to write the code yourself and try to do the things described.

As you write more and more code, you start developing good habits. You start noticing things. In your own coding you start to apply rules based on experience and learning. These can be things like noticing which structures in the code lead to later problems even if they are a good idea right now.

You also start to realise how you can implement certain structures which will give you greater freedom later to allow the code to evolve sensibly.

You start to lay down generalised and specific rules for yourself. In good coders these are second nature. Even great coders need to work new things through a few times in order to make it stick.

Because of the nature of coding and coders these rules migrate from one programmer to the next. They became really well formalised, in what developers call patterns.

Now, there are some meta rules that all coders learn early on. One such is not to repeat code. If you find yourself writing the same piece of code over and over again you generalise the logic and turn it into a function or a method. This allows you to have the code written in only one place but you can call it from many places in the program. The main advantages are:

✔ It saves time because the next time you need to do the same thing in your code, you have the function already written and you just have to call it.

✔ When you need to change it you do not have to look for all the instances of it throughout the code. You only have to change it in one place. The fixes and updates are applied to everything that uses it.

These are such general rules, that even someone who has never coded can understand them and the reason for thinking this way.

There are other rules that are more esoteric and specific. These are captured as refactorings. Martin Fowler wrote the seminal work on refactoring and as far as I know he remains the expert[85]. In the book he talks about recognising symptoms that tell you when you need to refactor code. He refers to these as bad smells in code. For example when one class is constantly calling the methods of another class, this is a smell that triggers a certain set of refactorings or remedial actions.

Outside coding we can apply a similar approach. People have layers of rules. These are less specific as they deal with a wider scope and more specific as they deal with a narrower scope.

Rules can be promoted and demoted as things happen to broaden the knowledge.

If this theory holds true then the rules should be internally consistent. Rules higher on the hierarchy should encapsulate all the rules beneath them.

---

85 Refactoring – Martin Fowler (Addison Wesley) **ISBN-13:** 978-0201485677

For example: Swans are white because I have never seen a black one. Oops there goes a black swan. Rule update, swans can be black or white. I better keep an eye out for other colours.

Some rules come from society. Most people reading this book would find it unacceptable to kill, steal, lie, cheat or bully. We don't need to. Furthermore we can see how these rules make a lot of sense in a civilised society or organisation.

There are other rules we decide on for ourselves as a result of our experience. We know that, as colleagues, we are more successful if we apply these rules to ourselves. Playing to other people's strengths is a good example.

We know that when we recognise and acknowledge the positive points of others, we give them confidence and they will like working with us. We also know that they will do a better job if it is something they know they have a reputation for doing well.

The more specific the rules get, the more detailed they get. The more detailed and specific rules are, the shorter their lifespan and scope.

We function this way. We do not want to have to figure everything out from first principles all the time. When we hear new things we measure them against our rules.

The problem with RULES

The relationships get inverted. Rather than updating the rules to mirror reality we start to distort reality to fit in with our rules. We delete things and we generalise at too low a level. We try to make a general rule out of a specific rule that is not really ready for promotion.

Context

Do you know a child you like and could talk to? Someone once said that everyone under the age of 2 is a genius. A scan of a normal two year old brain shows astonishing activity. The young brain is lit up. They are learning language, motor skills and how to interact with the world. They are learning about cause and effect and how to reason.

When I watch my own children learning I always notice how they can reinterpret the rules and create new rules in real time. This is pure genius.

If you open any book of philosophy it will advise you that we should strive for an inquisitive mind. Minds that become hardened to new experience become stale and become mistaken.

The world moves on. Entropy takes care of that. It also takes care of the fact that you can not isolate yourself from change and that there are few rules that are permanent.

We need to be able to generate new rules and refresh the old ones in the light of new experience as a matter of course. We need to recognise that we have distortions, deletions and inappropriate generalisations.

I was once in a team where there was a dispute over rules. One of the senior developers had her code reviewed by a more junior developer. The junior developer found that there was repeated code and he challenged the senior developer with the rule that you should never repeat code. The senior developer smiled and added "except where you need to". Her colleague thought she was making fun of him and insisted that the code should be rewritten.

The senior developer was not inclined to explain herself. I had a word with her privately about people skills and how to mentor junior colleagues.

Over a coffee we explained to the junior developer that the rule had been bent for a number of defensible reasons.

Primarily, a lot of code would have had to be redesigned in order to adhere to the rule. It was a stable part of the system with very few changes ever applied to the code. This meant that there was not much maintenance foreseen. The cost benefit in this case was strongly in favour of not fixing it when it was not broken.

The senior developer was aware of the rule but, with experience, had weighed it up and decided to break it under the circumstances. The rule was very important to the junior developer as a specific rule which was helping him produce better code. The senior developer had demoted it to a rule of thumb as she had the perspective of ability and experience that allowed more flexible judgement.

The moral of the story?

- ✔ It is important to know what the rules are.
- ✔ It is more important to know where they came from.
- ✔ It is most important to know how and when to apply them.

Moderation in everything including moderation

To Refine is to make something pure or improve something, especially by removing unwanted material.

To Reduce is to make something smaller in size, amount, degree and importance.

You do not want to reduce your rules by making them so rigid that they are useless. There will always be people who want to take away the facility for others to think and make decisions. Rules can not replace the creativity, innovation, intuition and dreams of people.

You may find it more productive to refine your rules. You can make them purer. You can add knowledge and experience. You are honest even if it hurts and you have to let go of a belief.

Successful business depends on people being innovative and creative. People need to dream to be innovative and creative. People need to be happy in order to dream. Successful business depends on your ability to give your people the space and environment to dream and to be happy.

There was once a working artist hired by a very important person to create statues and paintings. He was being paid by the hour. After a while the employer became suspicious that there were no deliveries or progress reports. He sent a spy to watch the workman. The spy reported that the scoundrel was spending his days either sitting in his workshop staring or walking around the city aimlessly.

In a fury the employer set up a meeting with his hapless employee and laid these charges at his feet. The fellow explained that he was working very hard. His employer almost had an embolism on the spot and demanded he explain himself. The artist explained that he had been staring for weeks at a chunk of marble looking for the statue in it and that he had been walking the markets and the meeting places in the town sketching hands and faces.

The marble became David, probably the most famous statue in the world. The sketches became the ceiling of the Sistine chapel. Probably the most famous ceiling in the world.

Context

People need new experience in order to refresh their rules. All rules and all revolutionaries become the status quo. Things will stagnate unless refreshed. We need to be careful that we do not become that which we set out to challenge.

Think of your house. When did you last paint the kitchen? Was it clean and sparkling, delightful to be in? Was that the last coat of paint it will ever need?

Standing still is retreating.

Here is how you advance.

- Keep asking questions
  - → of yourself
  - → of others
- Take your most dearly held beliefs and subject them to the harshest light you can, as often as you can. Do not shrink from what you see.
  - → Refine it.
- Talk to everyone as if they had a secret to tell you.
  - → Listen
- When something does not work, ask why.
  - → When something does work, ask why.
- Seek surprise and novelty
  - → SURPRISE is the bedrock of learning. You need to shock the mind out of its kitchen and slap on a new coat of paint.
  - → SURPRISE is the way we make things different so that we remember them. Anchor your abilities to the new and the amazing if you want to be new and amazing.

Ceiling wax

There is a reason why science and enlightenment have shown us the stars.

If you go to the British Museum you can walk about among the treasures of the world. There you will find the plunder of an empire. There you will find treasures beyond measure preserved for posterity. There appears to be a balance pulled from the past.

This magnificent building is a testament to all that is great in a race that at one time or another fought with everyone. Go to the main hall then look up. What you will see is light. Through an improbable latticework of glass and steel the grand hall is flooded with light which shines on the oldest and the newest works of human creation.

Sit and have a coffee and listen to the music of the voices of the world as it passes through to view its heritage. Think of all the eyes that have looked into the past to bring the present into focus.

A museum is a strange place. It is full of surprises as you realise they had scissors before they built the pyramids. You can feel the living that happened between the wars and the torments. You feel the surge of creativity and ingenuity of our shared past. It is hard to think of any of those exhibits being anything but our shared past, regardless of where they came from or where we come from.

Look up again at that ceiling. It curves toward the central column as you imagine spacetime curves into a star. As you look up at the ceiling you are reminded of balance, inspiration, hierarchy and interconnectedness.

There is structure. The structure supports context, scope, hierarchy, form and connection. What if reality were like this? What if reality were an infrastructure upon which we lay our theories and our dreams?

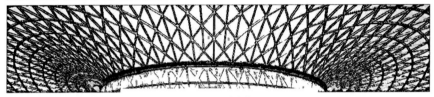

British Museum

Those principles which are laid upon the solid infrastructure hold fast. Principles laid upon those adhere. Principles laid across the spaces obscure the light.

When I first learned the principles of NLP I thought I understood. Then my great teachers told me that these were convenient lies and I was ready to understand. When I practised Agile I thought I had discovered principles and found a way to teach it through these bones. These too are convenient lies.

Metaphors are the greatest teaching tool to ever have been discovered and yet are nothing but convenient lies. All these conveniently lie upon the infrastructure of reality.

We can construct edifices to our arrogance but only those which lie, by design or by accident, upon the struts of truth will persist.

Why do you need things like NLP, Agile, Systems Thinking and the Theory of Constraints to be effective? I will tell you but first I will ask you to open your mind even more than it is already open. Delve deep into your untapped resources and find the strength to come up the hierarchy until you can see the world beneath you and your life spread out in spacetime.

Ceiling wax

See the lattice of reality clear of detail and clear of purpose. Look back at all those from whom you come. Contemplate the scientists, thinkers, artists and dreamers present, gone and yet to come. What are they constructing? Is it a map of the deep structure of possibility, perchance? Can it be that you are part of that great web?

Agile, NLP, Systems Thinking and their like are based on principles. The people who laid down their surface principles genuinely tried to lay them down on solid principles which they believed to be laid at some level on the deep structure. They were wise and humble enough to admit that there is more deep structure to be discovered.

Those things which are based on principle allow the light through and entertain enlightenment.

There are more principles which we must build on the infrastructure of reality if they are to hold true across the ceiling.

To use any tool effectively you must understand not just what it does but how it does it and why. A tool is only as good as the workman using it.

I have seen Michelangelo's ceiling twice in my life. I fell in love with it when I was twelve and I saw it again with my wife on our honeymoon.

The first time I saw the colour and the scope and the majesty of it; and I asked myself: "How did a man conceive of this? How did a human being make something like this from nothing?".

Ceiling wax

The second time I saw the same thing and I saw more. I saw that he had used the struts and vaults and architecture of the ceiling as part of his painting. On that map of his soul up there, he had used the supports that held up the ceiling to bind it.

Come back down and bring the view with you. Now look up at the ceiling again. See the connections.

Those people I know who are scientists have a difficult time explaining to those who do not care to understand. Scientists insist on empirical proof, repeatability, peer review and time. This can be mistaken for unwillingness to accept change. Nothing could be further from the truth for a true scientist.

They do this because they want to build change on solid principle and they are aware of those that have gone before and those who are to come.

I asked you at the outset will a wheel roll, will a lever move weights, will equality always balance, will distance change perspective, whether or not we have a peer review or a theory?

Yes it will and the peer review did not make it true. The peer review determined that, as far as they could tell, a new strut, a new connection had been discovered.

The first thing a scientist does is to dream and to create possibilities. He or she dreams of where a strut may be. In the beginning I observed that "Science is based on observation, the serendipity of observation and the patterns that emerge from it. Observation, hypothesis, test, review, confirmation, theory. Elegant.".

Ceiling wax

The first thing an artist does is dream. The first thing an entrepreneur does is dream. The first thing a project manager does is to envision an outcome, which is a type of dream.

Principle based approaches anchor those dreams to possibility. Effectiveness is the ability to make something happen. Making something happen relies on connecting to the deep structure and donning the trousers of reality.

END OF VOLUME ONE

Author Online

The website for this book is:

www.TrousersOfReality.com

Illustration Index

Illustration Index

Bibliography

Adams, Douglas - *Hitch Hikers Guide to the Galaxy* - Pan Books (1979)

Alexander, F. Matthias - *The Use of the Self* - E. P. Dutton (New York, 1932), republished by Orion Publishing (2001)

Asimov, Isaac – *Foundation* - Gnome Press (1951)

Bandler, Richard & Grinder, John - The Structure of Magic I: A Book About Language and Therapy - Palo Alto, CA: Science and Behavior Books (1975)

Beck, Kent - *Extreme Programming Explained: Embrace Change* - Addison-Wesley. (1999)

Burgess, Melvin – *Junk* - Andersen Press (1996)

Cockburn, Alistair - *Agile Software Development* - Addison-Wesley Professional (1st edition 2001)

Collins, Wilkie - *The Moonstone* - (1868)

Conan Doyle, Arthur - *The Adventures of Sherlock Holmes* - (1892)

Conan Doyle, Arthur - *The Return of Sherlock Holmes* - (1904)

De Bono, Edward - *Lateral Thinking: A Textbook of Creativity* - Penguin (new edited edition 1990)

De Marco, Tom & Lister Tim - *Peopleware : Productive Projects and Teams* - (1987)

Deming, W. Edwards - Out of the Crisis - MIT Press (1986).

Field, Tim - *Bully in Sight* - Success Unlimited (1996)

Fowler, Martin; Kent *Beck*, John Brant, William Opdyke, and Don Roberts - *Refactoring: Improving the Design of Existing Code* - Addison-Wesley (1999).

Gladwell, Malcolm – *Blink* - Back Bay Books, Little Brown (2005)

Gladwell, Malcolm - *The Tipping Point* - Little Brown (2000)

Gödel, Kurt - *On Formally Undecidable Propositions Of Principia Mathematica And Related Systems* - tr. Martin Hirzel 2000.

Goldratt, Eliyahu M. - *It's Not Luck"* - North River Press (1994)

Goldratt, Eliyahu M. , Cox, Jeff - The Goal: A Process of Ongoing Improvement - North River Press; 2nd Rev edition (1992).

Bibliography

Haidt, Jonathan - *The Happiness Hypothesis: Finding Modern Truth in Ancient Wisdom* - Basic Books (2005)

Hawkings, Stephen - *Brief History Of Time* - Bantam Press (1988)

Hofstadter, Douglas - *Godel, Escher, Bach* - Basic Books (1979)

Kohn, Alfie - *Punished by Rewards: The Trouble with Gold Stars, Incentive Plans, A's, Praise, and Other Bribes* - Houghton Mifflin (1993/1999)

Lao Tzu - *Tao Te Ching* - c. 6th century BC

Luft, J. and Ingham, H. - *The Johari window, a graphic model of interpersonal awareness, Proceedings of the western training laboratory in group development.*- Los Angeles: UCLA (1955)

Maslow, Abraham - *A Theory of Human Motivation* - Psychological Review 50(4) (1943):370-96.

McGregor, Douglas - *The Human Side of Enterprise* - 1960

Moore, Gordon E. - *Progress in digital integrated electronics* - (1975).

Newton, Isaac - *Philosophiæ Naturalis Principia Mathematica* - (1687)

Pinker, Stephen - The Blank Slate: The Modern Denial of Human Nature - (2002)

Pirsig, Robert M. - *Zen and the Art of Motorcycle Maintenance* - New York: Bantam Books (1974)

Plato - *The Republic* - c. 380 BC

Pratchett, Terry – *Sourcery* - Victor Gollancz (1988)

Strickland, Bill & Rause, Vince - *Make the Impossible Possible: One Man's Crusade to Inspire Others to Dream Bigger and Achieve the Extraordinary* - New York: Currency Books of Random House (2007)

Taylor , Frederick Winslow - *Principles of Scientific Management.*- New York and London, Harper & brothers (1911)

White, T.H. - *The Once and Future King* - HarperCollins (1958)

Whitehead, Alfred North & Russell, Bertrand - *Principia mathematica* - Cambridge: University Press, (1910)

Index

273

Index

Index

Index

Index

Index